FOR THE LOVE OF THE
ROYAL FAMILY

FOR THE LOVE OF THE ROYAL FAMILY

Summersdale Publishers Ltd
46 West Street
Chichester
West Sussex
PO19 1RP
UK

www.summersdale.com

Printed and bound in the Czech Republic

ISBN: 978-1-84953-926-5

Substantial discounts on bulk quantities of Summersdale books are available to corporations, professional associations and other organisations. For details contact Nicky Douglas by telephone: +44 (0) 1243 756902, fax: +44 (0) 1243 786300 or email: nicky@summersdale.com.

FOR THE LOVE OF THE
ROYAL FAMILY

A COMPANION

ROGER BRYAN

summersdale

CONTENTS

Introduction...7

SAXON KINGS..9
Egbert (802–839)...9
Ethelwulf (839–858)..10
Ethelbald (858–860)...11
Ethelbert (860–865)...12
Ethelred I (865–871)...12
Alfred the Great (871–899)..14
Edward the Elder (899–924)...17
Athelstan (924–939)..17
Edmund I (939–946)..18
Edred (946–955)...19
Edwy the Fair (955–959)...20
Edgar the Peaceful (959–975)...21
Edward the Martyr (975–978)...22
Ethelred II (978–1016)..23
Edmund II (1016)...25

DANISH KINGS OF ENGLAND...........................27
Cnut (1016–1035)...27
Harold I (1035–1040)..31
Hardecnut (1040–1042)..32

SAXON KINGS RESTORED.................................33
Edward the Confessor (1042–1066)......................................33
Harold II (1066)...35

HOUSE OF NORMANDY.....................................41
William I (1066–1087)...41

William II (1087–1100)..48
Henry I (1100–1135)...51
Stephen (1135–1154)...54

HOUSE OF PLANTAGENET.....................................57
Henry II (1154–1189)...57
Richard I (1189–1199)..61
John (1199–1216)...65
Henry III (1216–1272)...69
Edward I (1272–1307)..72
Edward II (1307–1327)...76
Edward III (1327–1377)...79
Richard II (1377–1399)..85

HOUSE OF LANCASTER...87
Henry IV (1399–1413)..87
Henry V (1413–1422)...89
Henry VI (1422–1461; 1470–1471)....................................93

HOUSE OF YORK...97
Edward IV (1461–1470; 1471–1483)..................................97
Edward V (1483)..98
Richard III (1483–1485)...100

HOUSE OF TUDOR...103
Henry VII (1485–1509)...103
Henry VIII (1509–1547)..107
Edward VI (1547–1553)...112
Mary I (1553–1558)..116
Elizabeth I (1558–1603)...118

HOUSE OF STUART..125
James I (1603–1625)...125

Charles I (1625–1649)..129
Charles II (1660–1685)..134
James II (1685–1688)...138

HOUSE OF ORANGE AND STUART.....................141
William III (1689–1702) and Mary II (1689–1694)...........141
Anne (1702–1714)..143

HOUSE OF HANOVER...147
George I (1714–1727)..147
George II (1727–1760)...150
George III (1760–1820)..153
George IV (1820–1830)..159
William IV (1830–1837)...162
Victoria (1837–1901)..165

HOUSE OF SAXE-COBURG AND GOTHA.............179
Edward VII (1901–1910)..179

HOUSE OF WINDSOR (FROM 1917)......................185
George V (1910–1936)...185
Edward VIII (1936)...192
George VI (1936–1952)..196
Elizabeth II (1952–)...201

Afterword...227
Acknowledgements...229
Select Bibliography..230

INTRODUCTION

The monarchy is the oldest institution in Britain, older indeed than the nation itself. More than 1,200 years ago, Egbert became the first English king. There have been 61 monarchs since and Queen Elizabeth II is a descendant of Egbert.

This account of the kings and queens of England is not a textbook, but I hope you'll find it informative and entertaining. It will help you brush up your names and dates, and will also help to fill in a few of those gaps that most of us have in our knowledge of British history. It may even give you some 'I never knew that' moments!

As Walter Bagehot once said, the royal family is the universal family – the living thread of national continuity. We can all identify with the royals and share their experiences of triumph and failure, and family life in general. While everybody will have different memories, the milestones of the royal family's lives help bring our own experiences into a shared context. For example, my mother would be two years older than the Queen if she were alive today, and I am a year older than Prince Charles.

I think my first conscious memory of anything is cutting articles and pictures from newspapers and putting them in a scrapbook for the Coronation in 1953, at the age of six. My path and the Queen's 'crossed' again during 1977 when I played bass guitar in a band in a field at a Silver Jubilee party in the Cotswolds.

Later I wrote a headline in the 1980s, for *The Mail on Sunday*, on a picture of the Queen at Trooping the Colour. It had been pouring down and the picture was a very tight close-up of Her Majesty on her horse with a raindrop hanging off the end of her nose. The headline was: 'Rain Too Long Over Us.' Corny, perhaps, but the editor and my colleagues liked it.

As in all families, life has had its ups and downs, but through it all, the Queen has been a steadfast representative of everything that makes Britain great. To return that headline writer's thought to its original form: Long to reign over us, God Save the Queen.

TECHNICAL NOTE:

There have been 61 monarchs since King Egbert. Sweyn Forkbeard (1013), Matilda (1141) and Lady Jane Grey (1553) ruled for short periods, but were never crowned and so are not considered monarchs. William III and Mary II count as two, first as joint monarchs, and then William on his own after Mary died. Neither Edward V (1483) nor Edward VIII (1936) were crowned, but as both were heirs apparent, they qualified for a squad number and are considered to be monarchs.

SAXON KINGS

EGBERT

*c.*770–839, reigned 802–839
Son of Ealhmund of Kent

Egbert is considered to be the first King of all England. Originally he was king of the West Saxons but was forced to move into exile at the court of Charlemagne during the rule of King Offa of Mercia.

Egbert returned home after Offa died, regaining his kingdom in 802 and established himself as King of Wessex. He conquered Kent and Cornwall before defeating the Mercians at the Battle of Ellandune near Swindon in 825, when he was acknowledged to be King of all England by the other Saxon kingdoms: he controlled all of England south of the Humber and was given the title of *Bretwalda*, Anglo-Saxon for the Ruler of the British.

He was married to Redburga and had three children. He was the grandfather of King Alfred and the 34th great-grandfather of Elizabeth II.

ETHELWULF

*c.*800–858, reigned 839–858
Son of Egbert and Redburga

Ethelwulf spent most of the time during his reign fighting Viking incursions, inflicting a famous victory against them at Oakley in Surrey, which at least gave him temporary respite. The *Anglo-Saxon Chronicle* describes the victory as 'the greatest slaughter of a heathen army that was ever heard of to this present day'.

His four sons with his first wife, Osburga, were brought up with a reverence for religion; at his request, the four sons were each to become king in turn, rather than risk the stability of the line caused by infighting between his younger children and the children of his eldest son.

He took his youngest and favourite son, Alfred, the future Great one, on a pilgrimage to Rome in 855. On the way back in 856, at the age of 56, Ethelwulf married 13-year-old Princess Judith, Emperor Charlemagne's granddaughter.

She was anointed and crowned queen by the Archbishop of Rheims; it was the first recorded coronation of an English queen.

When Ethelwulf returned back to England, his son Ethelbald was in revolt and the King was forced to share the throne with him. Ethelwulf died two years later and was regarded as one of most successful West Saxon kings, leaving a number of religious and charitable bequests: perhaps his most important legacy being the order of succession he formulated for his sons.

ETHELBALD

*c.*831–860, reigned 858–860
Son of Ethelwulf and Osburga

Ethelbald, like his father, was crowned at Kingston upon Thames. And like his father, he married Charlemagne's widowed granddaughter Judith, who was now 15 – and also inconveniently, his stepmother. The marriage shocked the church, which regarded the relationship as incestuous in direct contravention of church law.

Judith's first two husbands did not live long – Ethelbald died two and a half years after being married. Judith was a widow twice over at 17.

 ### WHAT'S IN A NAME?

Egbert = hard edge (sword)
Ethelwulf = noble wolf
Ethelbald = noble bold
Ethelbert = noble magnificent
Ethelred = noble counsel
Athelstan = noble stone

ETHELBERT

c.834–865, reigned 860–865
Son of Ethelwulf and Osburga

Ethelbert was made King of Kent in 858 and then King of Wessex when his brother Ethelbald died. His reign was marked by numerous Viking invasions; the city of Winchester was burned to the ground in 860. The Danes created havoc in the south and east during this time, mounting merciless raids of pillage, slaughter and rape, leaving despair, destruction and devastation in their wake.

When Ethelbert died in 865, although he left a son Ethelwald and other children, he was succeeded on the throne by his younger brother Ethelred, as decreed by their father, Ethelwulf.

ETHELRED I

c.837–871, reigned 865–871
Son of Ethelwulf and Osburga

Ethelred I was a pious man who took the throne just as England was being ravaged by the largest Viking invasion so far, in 865 and 866.

Halfdan Ragnarsson and Ivar the Boneless landed in East Anglia with what was described as 'a great heathen army' and quickly proceeded to take York, establishing the Viking kingdom of Jorvik in 867. Halfdan became the first King of York.

The invasion was turning into occupation; from the Tees to the Thames, England became known as Danelaw. Spurred on by their successes, the Vikings prepared to attack Wessex. They were met in 870 by Ethelred I and his brother Alfred at the Battle of Ashdown in Oxfordshire. The Saxons were victorious after a violent pitched battle.

Ethelred I's piety was held in great esteem and he was venerated as a saint; before the Battle of Ashdown, he refused to rise from his knees until he had finished hearing the Mass. He said he would not serve man before God. Ethelred was to die of injuries suffered at the Battle of Merton a year later.

 IVAR THE BONELESS

There is much disagreement as to the meaning of Ivar's puzzling epithet 'the Boneless'. He was a man of exceptional cruelty and ferocity (which is saying something for a Viking warrior) and it's thought that he was so called because he had a medical condition that caused his legs to fracture easily. Not one to let broken legs stand in the way of a good fight, Ivar had his men carry him into battle on a shield and fought with bow and arrow.

It has also been suggested that Boneless was a euphemism for impotence. The sagas say that 'neither love nor lust played any part' in Ivar's life, and he died childless, so perhaps his nickname was not connected to his fearsome reputation on the battlefield, after all. He was a bona fide warrior.

ALFRED THE GREAT

*c.*849–899, reigned 871–899
Son of Ethelwulf and Osburga

Alfred was widely adjudged to be an outstanding king, fully deserving the moniker 'Great'. His three elder brothers had all been Saxon kings and, as a young boy, he travelled twice to Rome, so he had some inside knowledge of monarchy and religion and European culture by the time he became king when he was 22.

He was a warrior king, like all Anglo-Saxon kings. He fought a number of fierce battles with his older brother Ethelred to defeat the Danes, and became king after Ethelred was killed at the Battle of Merton. But he was also what could be described as a philosopher king. He learned Latin and wrote many treatises.

The Danes were moving further and further west at the start of his reign. For three years King Guthrum was on the march, pillaging all over Wessex.

❧ ALFRED AND THE BURNT CAKES

It was early in his reign that the story of Alfred and the burnt cakes appeared – a story that may well be an invention, but is better remembered than some of his real and substantial achievements.

In January 878, Alfred was taken by surprise when Guthrum attacked Chippenham and he had to flee. He was forced to go into hiding in the Somerset Levels near Athelney; this is where the famous episode of the burnt cakes is supposed to have happened.

Alfred and his men were hiding in the marshes, dependent on the locals for food and shelter. Disguised as an ordinary traveller, Alfred was staying in a peasant's cottage and was asked to keep his eye on some cakes (probably bread – it wasn't *The Great British Bake Off*) cooking by the fire. Deep in thought, perhaps, on matters of state and how he was going to save Wessex and regain power, he let the cakes burn. The swineherd's wife came back and severely scolded him for his inattention, not knowing his identity.

The story is a legend but a completely believable one. It is dated and located at a real place where we know Alfred was at that time. And with the future of Wessex in the balance, he surely had more important things to think about than a few cakes on the fire. The King could easily have pulled rank and said something along the lines of 'Do you know who I am?' Instead, to his credit, he accepted the peasant's rebuke with grace and humility.

THE BATTLE OF EDINGTON

One of the most important battles in English history was the Battle of Edington, near Chippenham in Wiltshire in May 878. Had the Danes won, Danelaw would have extended all over Wessex.

The battle was one of the great turning points of English history. The hand-to-hand fighting with swords and axes was ferocious and went on for hours. The Danes were decisively beaten and Alfred followed them back to their camp near Bath and surrounded them. They were at his mercy.

He insisted that the Danish leader Guthrum, along with 30 of his warriors, be baptised as Christians with Alfred as the Viking king's godfather, which made him a dependant.

It is said he then entertained the Danish troops for almost two weeks and showered gifts on them. He then let them go – and enjoyed 14 years of peace.

66 ·

I pause to think with admiration
of the noble king, who in his single
person, possessed all the Saxon virtues;
whom misfortune could not subdue,
whom prosperity could not spoil, whose
perseverance nothing could shake; who was
hopeful in defeat, and generous in success; who
loved justice, freedom, truth and knowledge.

CHARLES DICKENS ON ALFRED THE GREAT IN
A CHILD'S HISTORY OF ENGLAND, 1851.

· ·

⚜ ALFRED'S INFLUENCE

Alfred was an innovative peacetime ruler: he reorganised the defences of Wessex, establishing a sort of rota system for military service, which meant that at any one time, he effectively had a standing army. He strengthened fortresses and built strategically placed new ones – these were boroughs (in Saxon *burgh* means fortress). He built large, fast ships to fight the Danes and is sometimes called the father of the English navy.

He also revised the laws of the land and generally encouraged learning – he himself made a number of translations from and into Latin. On coins, he was described as *rex Anglorum* (King of the English). In 890, he commissioned the *Anglo-Saxon Chronicle*, which became a fount of knowledge for the period.

He died at the age of 50 and had rightly earned the epithet 'the Great'.

EDWARD THE ELDER

870–924, reigned 899–924
Son of Alfred and Elswitha

The son of Alfred the Great, he fought successfully against the Danes, capturing the boroughs of Leicester, Stamford, Nottingham, Derby and Lincoln. In 901, he took the title King of the Angles and Saxons.

Edward the Elder married three times and fathered 18 legitimate children: he had two sons and a daughter with Egwina; ten children by Elfleda; and five more by Edgifu. Oh, and it was rumoured that he had an illegitimate son in Germany. No problem with the succession there then.

ATHELSTAN

c.895–939, reigned 924–939
Son of Edward and Egwina

Athelstan was a tall and handsome youth with light flaxen hair, and a favourite of his grandfather King Alfred. He was an audacious soldier and was said never to have lost a battle.

He was crowned King of the Anglo-Saxons in 924 and became King of England from 927 until his death in 939. He was the first undisputed king of all England, ruling Wessex and Mercia – the Welsh and Scottish also paid homage to him. His realm was roughly equivalent to the present area of England. Athelstan arranged advantageous marriages for his sister and stepsisters, administered the country with great skill and introduced a national coinage; it is fitting that he should be the first King of England to be depicted (on coins) wearing a crown.

Athelstan died at the height of his power and was buried at Malmesbury; a church charter of 934 described him as 'King of the English, elevated by the right hand of the Almighty... to the Throne of the whole Kingdom of Britain'.

William of Malmesbury wrote of him, 200 years later, 'The firm opinion is still current among the English that no one more just or learned administered the state.'

He remained unmarried and was succeeded by his half-brother Edmund.

EDMUND I (EDMUND THE ELDER)

*c.*921–946, reigned 939–946
Son of Edward and Edgifu

Edmund was crowned at Kingston upon Thames when he was only 18. His was a short life – he was 25 when he was involved in a brawl and stabbed to death in Gloucestershire. He married twice; his two sons, Edwy and Edgar, from his first marriage to Elgifu were later to become kings. His brother Edred succeeded him.

SEVEN KINGS AND A LOT OF CARS

The Kingston upon Thames Coronation Stone is a sarsen stone (a sandstone block) used at the coronation of seven Saxon kings. It was originally in the Church of St Mary, which collapsed in 1730, and is now located next to the Guildhall in the High Street. The seven kings were: Edward the Elder, Athelstan, Edmund, Edred, Edwy, Edward the Martyr and Ethelred. Apart from its obvious homage, the Seven Kings multi-storey car park in Kingston is of very limited historical or architectural interest.

EDRED

923–955, reigned 946–955
Son of Edward and Edgifu

A small and slightly built man, Edred suffered from a form of wasting disease that eventually killed him. His main enemy during his reign was Eric Bloodaxe who had become the Viking king of Northumbria and some years later, King of York. Eric was to be the last Viking King of York. Edred defeated his bloodthirsty rival, who was killed in battle in 954.

Edred was a supporter of the monastic reform movement. Advised by St Dunstan, Abbot of Glastonbury, who was to become a much-loved Archbishop of Canterbury, he helped to establish religious centres of learning. In his later years, as his health deteriorated, Edred delegated much work to St Dunstan.

EDWY THE FAIR

*c.*940–959, reigned 955–959
Son of Edmund I and Elgifu

Edwy's life was a short one and many people said, mercifully so. He was crowned king when he was just 15, and murdered when he was 19. A good-looking youth by all accounts, he much preferred a fair lady's bedchamber to the boring council chamber. Dunstan was frequently angered by his behaviour and admonished him. Edwy infamously left his coronation banquet in Kingston upon Thames to cavort on a bed with his mistress (Elgifu, his stepsister) and – to make matters worse – his equally amorous stepmother (Ethelgifu). A chronicler describes Edwy 'repeatedly wallowing between the two of them in evil fashion, as if in a vile sty' and Edwy was marched back to be rebuked by Archbishop Odo. He did end up marrying his mistress but the marriage was adjudged to be illegal, since the two were related.

Dunstan was forced out of the country, fleeing for his life before finding refuge in Ghent. Edwy lost control of Mercia and Northumbria, and was forced to give up the throne to his brother Edgar before he was murdered in 959.

ERIC BLOODAXE

The son of Harald Finehair, Eric Bloodaxe established himself as ruler of the Viking kingdom of Northumbria around 950. He features in a number of sagas and like his near contemporary, Thorfinn Skullsplitter of Orkney, conjures up a terrifying image of a Viking warrior: big, bearded, brave and in possession of a very large and sharp axe.

Harald's kingdom was not sufficient to provide much of an inheritance for his many sons, so Eric secured the succession for himself by gradually murdering all his brothers in turn. That's one way of taking over the family business – he well deserved his nickname.

EDGAR THE PEACEFUL

*c.*943–975, reigned 959–975
Son of Edmund I and Elgifu

The son of Edmund the Elder and Elgifu, Edgar brought much needed stability and prosperity to the realm. He chose his advisers wisely: St Dunstan, whom he brought back from exile in Belgium to be Bishop of Worcester, then London and, later still, Archbishop of Canterbury in 961 and St Oswald, who was made Archbishop of York. A deeply pious man, he founded 40 religious houses.

Edgar delayed his coronation until 973 and St Dunstan devised a service that featured the anointing of the monarch, with the words from 1 Kings 1:38–40, 'Zadok the Priest and Nathan the Prophet anointed Solomon King'. The same service has been used at coronations ever since. After his coronation and in a piece of PR that spin doctors today would be proud of, he summoned eight sub-kings of Britain for a meeting on the River Dee. In a demonstration of Wessex power, Edgar was rowed up the Dee by the sub-kings and attended by a large number of nobles. It was the embodiment of the Saxon supremacy over the Celts of England, Scotland and Wales.

EDWARD THE MARTYR

*c.*963–978, reigned 975–978
Son of Edgar I and Ethelfled

Edward became king when he was 12 and reigned for less than three years – murdered at Corfe, Dorset, by his brother Ethelred's retainers, possibly on the orders of his stepmother, Elfrida.

Edward's death led to a rapid growth of his cult and he became known as a saint and a martyr. Miracles were said to have occurred at his tomb at Wareham and it was decided to move his body to Shaftesbury Abbey. The cortege took seven days to cover the 25 miles and more miracles were said to have occurred en route. The *Anglo-Saxon Chronicle* describes Edward as a heavenly saint.

Pilgrims still visit his modern shrine at Brookwood Cemetery near Woking.

ETHELRED II (ETHELRED THE UNREADY)

*c.*968–1016, reigned 978–1016
Son of Edgar I and Elfrida

Ethelred II was crowned king when he was ten after the murder of his half-brother Edward by his supporters.

The epithet Unready is derived from *unraed*, meaning 'no counsel' or 'ill-advised', and puns on his name, Ethelraed, which means 'noble counsel'. Ethelraed Unraed = Noble counsel, No counsel. The first recorded use of the nickname was 150 years after his death.

Ethelred tried to buy off the Danes and Vikings with huge amounts of money levied through a tax called *Danegeld*, a strategy that certainly was ill-advised. In 1002, in a change of policy, he ordered the massacre of all Danes in England on St Brice's Day, 13 November. This too was ill-advised. It would hardly have been possible to murder all the Danes. Maybe the decree applied only to more recent arrivals, but whether the government was capable of organising a mass killing effectively is in considerable doubt. But one thing it did do was upset the Danes greatly (which was certainly ill-advised). In 1006, the *Anglo-Saxon Chronicle* reported: 'in spite of it all, the Danish Army went as it pleased.'

Ethelred had 13 children with his first wife, Elfled, and three others with his second wife, Emma of Normandy, one of whom was Edward, later known as the Confessor. Eventually Ethelred had to flee the country in 1013, when Sweyn Forkbeard first invaded England. Although he was never crowned, Sweyn ruled England for a short time before his death in 1014; Ethelred returned, but he himself died in 1016.

 LAID TO REST IN WINCHESTER

Winchester Cathedral is the resting place of some of the earliest kings of England; their remains are said to be contained in six beautifully decorated mortuary chests. The chests are inscribed but they were made hundreds of years after the original burials in the old minster.

Among those whose remains are thought to be in the chests are the first English King Egbert (802–839), King Ethelwulf (839–859), King Edred (946–955), King Edwy (955–959), King Cnut (1016–1035) and his wife, Emma of Normandy, who died in 1052.

Historical records indicate that their bones were placed in the mortuary chests around the St Swithun's Shrine above the high altar of the cathedral in the 12th century.

They survived destruction at the time of the Dissolution of the Monasteries but in 1642, at the beginning of the Civil War, the Roundheads ran amok in the cathedral. The mortuary chests were broken open and the remains scattered. A cleric, writing in 1643, described how Cromwell's soldiers smashed the Cathedral windows by throwing the bones from the chests of 'Kings, Queens, Bishops, Confessors and Saints'.

Following the attack the remains were gathered together and placed back into six of the chests. They were muddled up by then with no way of knowing which bones were which.

Work started in 2015 in examining the bone fragments using radiocarbon dating and preliminary tests by a team from Oxford University show that the remains are from the late Anglo-Saxon and early Norman periods, which is consistent with the historical burial records. The work is still going on.

EDMUND II (EDMUND IRONSIDE)

*c.*992–1016, reigned Apr–Nov 1016
Son of Ethelred II and Elfled

His nickname describes his strength. He was crowned in April 1016 and died that November, probably murdered. He had some success fighting the Danes, but lost a decisive battle at Ashingdon in Essex, and was forced to partition the country, sharing it with Sweyn Forkbeard's son Cnut. Edmund died soon after and the throne was left completely to the Danes led by King Cnut.

DANISH KINGS
OF ENGLAND

CNUT (CANUTE)

c.992–1035, reigned 1016–1035
Son of Sweyn Forkbeard and
Gunhild of Poland

Younger son of Sweyn, he accompanied his father on the invasion that led to the Danish conquest of 1013. After his father's death, Cnut retreated to Denmark, returning in 1015 to challenge Ethelred the Unready and Edmund Ironside for the throne of England.

It was a serious invasion – he mustered 20,000 troops and 22 longships. A year of fierce warfare followed – first London fell, then all of Wessex, Mercia and Northumbria.

SWEYN FORKBEARD

Tolkien couldn't have come up with a better name for a murderous Viking warlord. King of Denmark from 988, taking over from his father Harald Bluetooth, he spent most of his life attacking England, raising *Danegeld* and exploiting the weaknesses of King Ethelred II.

In 1013, he landed at Gainsborough, laying waste a wide area from Oxford and Winchester to London – women were burned alive, children impaled on lances, and men hung up to die suspended by their private parts. Ethelred fled to Normandy and Sweyn Forkbeard was duly declared King of all England on Christmas Day 1013 with Gainsborough as its capital.

He returned triumphantly to his fleet at Gainsborough soon after, but tragedy struck – he died there suddenly five weeks later and was never crowned. His son Cnut succeeded him.

DID YOU KNOW?

Sweyn Forkbeard's father, Harald Bluetooth (*c*.910–987), gave his name – posthumously – to the short-range wireless technology standard for exchanging data that was developed in the 1990s.

Scandinavian telecom companies Ericsson, Intel and Nokia were looking to create a universal standard. In December 1996, at a meeting of the interested parties in Lund, Sweden, Jim Kardach of Intel suggested the name Bluetooth. He had recently read a historical novel involving Harald Bluetooth (who had a prominent blue/black bad tooth) and explained that the 10th-century King of Denmark was famous for uniting Scandinavia just as they (the interested telecom companies) intended to unite the PC and cellular industries with a single wireless standard.

The Bluetooth logo merges the Nordic runes H (*hagall*, looks like an X) and B (*berkanen*) – the initials of Harold Bluetooth.

⚜ CNUT'S INFLUENCE

Cnut forced Edmund to partition the country, and he became King of all England on Edmund's death in 1016 very shortly (and very conveniently for Cnut) after the agreement had been signed. The next year, he married Ethelred the Unready's widow, Emma of Normandy. They had three children, one of whom, Hardecnut, was to become king in 1040. He spent most of his time in England living in Winchester although he was made King of Denmark in 1019 and King of Norway in 1028.

Cnut made his mark early on. Saxon malcontents were ruthlessly dealt with, and punitive taxes were imposed. According to the *Anglo-Saxon Chronicle*, Cnut put the recently deceased Forkbeard's hostages ashore at Sandwich in 1014 minus 'hands, ears and noses'.

Cnut then developed qualities of statesmanship – he paid off the Danish army and sent them home – and became a wise, strong and popular king, bringing stability to the country while maintaining good relations with the continent.

He acquired a reputation as a devout and pious Christian – partly due to the expert spin-doctoring of his bishops. It is not clear whether Cnut had married Elfgifu in 1015, but he publicly maintained two consorts after he married Emma of Normandy in 1017.

Cnut and Elfgifu's son Harold succeeded his father as king in 1035, and Hardecnut, his son by Emma, succeeded Harold in 1040. Cnut died at Shaftesbury and his bones lie in Winchester Cathedral.

⚜ THE STORY OF THE TIDE

The event that will forever be associated with Cnut is the story of the waves. King Cnut is reputed to have taken his courtiers to the beach in an attempt to stop the tide coming in.

The first written account of the Cnut episode was in *Historia Anglorum* (The History of the English People) by chronicler Henry of Huntingdon in the 12th century.

In Huntingdon's account, Cnut set his throne by the seashore and commanded the incoming tide to halt and not wet his feet and robes. Yet

> continuing to rise as usual [the tide] dashed over his feet and legs without respect to his royal person. Then the king leapt backwards, saying: 'Let all men know how empty and worthless is the power of kings, for there is none worthy of the name, but He whom heaven, earth, and sea obey by eternal laws.'

He then hung his gold crown on a crucifix, and never wore it again 'to the honour of God the almighty King'.

The account shows Cnut setting out to demonstrate that despite being an all-powerful monarch and despite what his fawning courtiers were telling him, he could not hold back the tide.

But it got twisted along the way and most modern-day telling of the Cnut story turns the account on its head suggesting that a deluded King Canute really did think he could hold back the tide.

HAROLD I (HAROLD HAREFOOT)

1016–1040, reigned 1035–1040
Son of Cnut and Elfgifu

Harold I's cognomen described his fleetness of foot and his skill as a hunter. Cnut had wanted his son with Emma, Hardecnut, to be king. However, while Hardecnut was away in Denmark, Cnut's first son, Harold, seized the throne. His reign, however, was not a happy one; it was short and brutish and he died aged 24 – according to one Saxon account, due to an illness brought on by divine judgment.

HARDECNUT

c.1018–1042, reigned 1040–1042
Son of Cnut and Emma
of Normandy

Hardecnut was crowned King of Denmark as Cnut III in 1035 and reigned until 1042. He became King of England when his brother Harold died in 1040. Hardecnut literally means 'Deadly Cnut'; in fact, it appears that he was a 'Thoroughly Nasty Cnut'. Almost the first thing he did when he arrived back in England was to dig up the body of his half-brother Harold Harefoot, buried at Westminster, behead it and throw it into a ditch; he then burned down the city of Worcester; and plundered and taxed his people to excess.

In 1041, he invited his mother, Emma of Normandy's, son Edward – his half-brother – back from exile in Normandy and made him his heir. A year later, he suffered a stroke during a drinking bout at a wedding and died shortly thereafter. Hardecnut was the last Scandinavian King of England.

SAXON KINGS RESTORED

EDWARD THE CONFESSOR

1004–1066, reigned 1042–1066
Son of Ethelred II and
Emma of Normandy

Edward is one of the most important monarchs in English history, although neither a warrior nor a statesman. He founded Westminster Abbey, where all coronations since have taken place, and established Westminster Palace, on the site of the present seat of government, choosing to make it his London home.

He was the product of mixed cultures: his father, Ethelred the Unready, was Saxon and his mother, Emma, Norman. When Ethelred died and Emma remarried – to King Cnut – Emma kept Edward well out of the way and had him brought up in her native Normandy. Edward was born a Saxon, but his upbringing was Norman.

With the support of Earl Godwin, Edward was able to return to England in 1041 and was crowned king in the following year. He was seen as something of an oddity – he had a very red face, and white skin, hair and beard, and he seemed more fitted for religious life than regal life. The name he was given by the people – Confessor – suggests he was seen more as a priest than a king. He was regarded as the patron saint of England for more than 400 years.

He swore a vow of chastity and was believed to have refused to consummate his marriage in 1045 with Edith, daughter of Earl Godwin.

⚜ A SOFT-HANDED RULER

Unsurprisingly on his return to England, he brought with him a number of his Norman friends and courtiers. William of Normandy was his great-nephew and a good friend, and it appears that in 1051, Edward made a promise to William that he would be his heir.

Edward left the business of government to others. He surrounded himself with his French-speaking advisers and was, to all intents and purposes, the first Norman King of England. English state documents were now written in French.

Edward lived to see the completion of Westminster Abbey but was too ill to attend the opening ceremony on 28 December 1065. He died a few days later, and fittingly must have been the first person to have been buried there.

He was made a saint in 1161. Henry III, who venerated Edward, was responsible in 1269 for what was at the time the most finely decorated shrine in Christendom. Thousands of pilgrims visited it every year.

Edward the Confessor was the great-great-great-grandson of King Alfred, stepson of King Cnut and great-uncle of the first

Norman king William the Conqueror. He had taken the English monarchy to the crossroads of history.

But he did not leave an heir, and on his death the matter of the succession was still to be settled.

 A WOLF IN SHEEP'S CLOTHING

Edward was well-known for standing with 'lamb-like meekness and tranquil mind at the holy offices of the masses'. It comes as something of a surprise therefore to find he spent much of his time in the pleasures of hunting. After a religious service that he attended every day, he took much pleasure in hawks and birds of that kind and was really 'delighted by the baying and scrambling of the hounds'.

HAROLD II

*c.*1020–1066, reigned Jan–Oct 1066
Son of Godwin, Earl of Wessex,
and Gytha

King Edward the Confessor was buried in Westminster Abbey on 6 January 1066, the day after he died. Immediately after the funeral, with breathtaking haste, Harold Godwinson was crowned King Harold II at the Abbey.

Harold's claim to the throne was that he was Edward's brother-in-law, and Edward is said to have named him heir on his deathbed. There were three other claimants: Edgar the Atheling, (a very young descendant of Ethelred II), King Harald Hardrada, King of Norway, and William, Duke of Normandy.

In 1051, the childless Edward had made a promise to his nephew Duke William that he would be heir. He then sent Harold to Normandy in 1064 for the purpose, it is said, of confirming Edward's promise of succession to William. Harold's trip started badly: he was shipwrecked off the French coast and captured. The Bayeux Tapestry records the drama, and also that William rushed to Harold's rescue. Later at William's palace at Rouen, Harold swore a very public oath to the duke – in reality he did not have any choice – promising to protect William's claim.

Harold has been captured for posterity making that promise on the Bayeux Tapestry – a propaganda coup for the Normans as this greatly helped to legitimise their conquest: '*Ubi Harold Sacramentum Fecit Willelmo Duci*' ('Where Harold took an oath to Duke William').

Back in England after Edward had died, the speed with which Harold was crowned, and the oath he had sworn to God in Normandy, gave some cause for alarm. People waited anxiously to see what God's reaction to all this would be.

BLAZING A TRAIL

Towards the end of April 1066, a huge streak of fire could be seen in the London night sky for seven nights in a row. Priests offered special prayers for safety and prophets foretold doom. What people did not realise was that the streak of fire, described by the Anglo-Saxon Chronicle as a 'hairy star', was in fact Halley's Comet on one of its 76-year periodic visits near earth. It was widely seen as an omen: William thought it was a good omen for him, and the comet was included on the Bayeux Tapestry, with Harold looking very worried.

THE BATTLE OF STAMFORD BRIDGE

In the summer of 1066, Harold began to receive reports that William in the south and Hardrada in the north were preparing independently to invade and take the crown. Harold's younger brother Tostig was planning to join forces with the Norwegians. Hardrada struck first – on 19 September, he sailed up the River Ouse with 300 ships, possibly the largest fleet ever to sail from Scandinavia. They plundered the local towns and villages and marched on to take the city of York.

Harold mobilised his army in the south of England very quickly and marched north to reach York a few days later. He found that Hardrada had assembled his men seven miles east of York and on 25 September, the bloody Battle of Stamford Bridge was fought. Hardrada and Tostig were both killed, along with most of their army. Fewer than 40 Viking ships were able to return home.

The victory was greater in scale than any battles won by Alfred and Athelstan, the most magnificent of all the victories against the Vikings.

 A BRIDGE TOO FAR

The English advance was delayed at one stage by a bottleneck on a bridge. A folk story has it that a giant Norse axeman blocked the narrow crossing over the River Derwent, and single-handedly held up the entire English army. The *Anglo-Saxon Chronicle* states that the axeman cut down up to 40 Englishmen. He was only stopped when an intrepid English soldier floated under the bridge on a makeshift raft and thrust his spear upwards through the laths in the bridge, mortally wounding the axeman. Ouch!

THE BATTLE OF HASTINGS

While he was celebrating this victory, Harold got news that William of Normandy had already landed on the south coast. This must have been utterly devastating for Harold: he had just marched 200 miles north from London and been involved in an extremely bloody battle, and now had to march back south as quickly as possible. He did it in four days, and then regrouped for another march, only 60 miles this time, further south to meet William near Hastings.

William brought a fleet of around 500 ships and landed at Pevensey Bay on the Sussex coast. Harold's fleet was stationed west of the Isle of Wight so the Normans landed unopposed – William confronted Harold at a place now called Battle.

The Battle of Hastings was a turning point. Everyone knows its date – 1066 – and everyone knows the outcome. Harold's troops were exhausted and England was conquered.

The battle is pictured in detail on the Bayeux Tapestry. Harold was struck down by an arrow in his eye but the sanitised version, as shown on the tapestry, may not tell the whole truth.

William had ordered a hit squad to kill the English king; a group of knights tracked Harold down and cut off his head and disembowelled him. According to Guy of Amiens, who reported on the battle in the following year, another knight tried to cut off one of Harold's legs. The standard battlefield mutilation at the time was full emasculation. Bishop Guy was almost certainly being euphemistic when he said Harold's leg was cut off.

Harold's body was so badly mutilated that he could not be identified; Edith of the Swan Neck, his common-law wife, had to be taken to the battlefield to identify his body from marks that only she knew. She unfastened his chainmail and uncovered the tattoo 'Edith and England' over his heart.

This was the last successful invasion of Britain by a foreign enemy: William had indeed conquered. In his estimation, Harold did not merit a royal burial and his body was left under a pile of stones on the clifftop near the spot where he fell. The grave was moved later to Waltham Abbey. Here endeth the line of the Saxon kings.

HOUSE OF NORMANDY

WILLIAM I (WILLIAM THE CONQUEROR)

1028–1087, reigned 1066–1087
Son of Robert I, Duke of Normandy,
and Arlette

The Norman conquest had begun at Hastings but it did not end there. William and his army faced fierce opposition from English nobles as they marched in a slash-and-burn campaign up to London for his coronation on Christmas Day, 1066.

William was far from secure and was reported to be shaking with fear when he was crowned king. Cries of adulation inside Westminster Abbey were interpreted by Norman soldiers outside as some sort of rebellion. The Norman guard then set fire to the Saxon dwellings near the abbey. According to the 12th-century Anglo-Norman historian Orderic Vitalis, William was left trembling.

William was descended from a long line of Viking warlords who settled in north-western France in the 9th century. He was a bastard, the illegitimate and only son of Robert and Arlette, the teenage daughter of a Normandy tanner.

He inherited the Duchy of Normandy when he was only seven years old and his struggle for survival helped to mould a resolute character; by the mid-1040s he was in a position to assert his own authority. He had become a hard and ruthless man.

William married his cousin Matilda, the daughter of Count Baldwin of Flanders, in 1053; they had four sons and six daughters. Their courtship was unconventional, to say the least. William had fallen in love with her but she had turned down his offer of marriage on the grounds that she was the daughter of a count and he was the illegitimate son of the Duke of Normandy.

William visited the palace of Count Baldwin at Lille and confronted the diminutive Matilda (who was less than five feet tall), furiously dragging her to the ground by her long hair and beating her mercilessly.

Matilda's father was furious with William, but probably not as furious as a few days later when Matilda, still recovering from the attack, said she would marry nobody but William.

How did she come to change her mind so quickly? She is reported to have said, 'I did not know the duke then so well as I do now; for he must be a man of great courage and high daring who could venture to come and beat me in my father's palace.' Well, that's one way of looking at it.

William had long had a plan to invade England, ever since his great-uncle Edward the Confessor gave him a promise in 1051 that he would be heir. This was backed up by Harold promising the English throne to William in 1064 in the famous scene on the Bayeux Tapestry. He must have felt doubly justified in making his plans.

William took a risk invading England – Harold was a capable and courageous military leader and had it not been for the attack by Hardrada in the north, he could well have been triumphant. But William's victory at Hastings set in motion wholesale changes for the Anglo-Saxon ruling classes.

 THE BAYEUX TAPESTRY

The Bayeux Tapestry is a historical and visual record of the Norman conquest – effectively, an embroidered newspaper report from the time.

The story starts in 1064 when Edward the Confessor sent his brother-in-law Harold to Normandy to tell William Duke of Normandy that he, William, had been named by Edward as his successor to the throne of England.

Harold prays in Bosham Church before leaving England. On his crossing, he is shipwrecked.

Harold famously swears fealty to William; Edward is buried; Harold is crowned; a comet appears; William loads his boats, sets sail, lands at Pevensey and wins the Battle of Hastings with Harold killed by an arrow in his eye. The whole story is there.

The tapestry is 70 metres long and 50 centimetres in height and embroidered on linen. It contains about 50 different scenes and one researcher has counted 632 human figures in it, 202 horses, 55 dogs, 505 other creatures (some clearly mythical beasts), 37 buildings, 41 ships, 49 trees and nearly 2,000 Latin letters. It is on permanent display in Bayeux.

FOR THE LOVE OF THE ROYAL FAMILY

> It is probable that the man who commissioned the tapestry was Bishop Odo of Bayeux, William's half-brother; his cathedral in Bayeux was consecrated in 1077. Where the tapestry was made and who made it is not clear, but one theory is that it was done by women in Canterbury, Kent, where there was a famous school of tapestry that produced work in a similar style.
>
> After William's victory at Hastings, Odo was made Earl of Kent, so it is not inconceivable that he would have known about this particular school. Another clue is that some of the names in Latin on the tapestry are not spelled in the way a French person would have written them but rather spelled in the English style of the time.
>
> The tapestry also shows how the two sides can be differentiated – by their haircuts. The English have shoulder-length hair and moustaches, while the Normans are clean-shaven and have their hair razor-cut dramatically high at the back.

⚜ MAKING HIS MARK

Having taken control of England, William ensured his success by putting down all opposition relentlessly and ruthlessly; the Saxon nobility was destroyed and almost totally dispossessed. The same happened to the church.

The Normans were great builders and a programme of building castles and cathedrals soon began, including William's biggest venture: the Tower of London. He also started to build Windsor

Castle, choosing the site himself (although he can't have known it would later be on the Heathrow flight path).

Castles were a physical representation of power. Unlike Alfred's *burghs*, which had been built to protect the population, William's castles were built for the opposite reason – to repress the locals. Castles were built at Cambridge, Warwick, Nottingham, Lincoln, York and many other places. Many survive today. The Normans extended their territories in Wales, building castles at Chepstow, Cardiff, Pembroke, Cardigan and Rhuddlan.

William built a new cathedral at Winchester alongside the old Saxon one and was re-crowned there every year just to remind everyone who was in charge. He also cleared woodland near Winchester for the New Forest – his own hunting ground.

Local opposition was quickly put down. The most serious campaign was the Harrying of the North in 1069–1070. William's army moved through Northumbria burning villages and farmland, and slaughtering locals. All farmland and property between York and Durham was devastated. One estimate was that up to 100,000 people starved to death in its aftermath.

The Harrying may have had the desired effect but there is evidence to suggest that William may have deeply regretted the severity of his actions. According to Orderic Vitalis, William bared all on his deathbed:

> *I persecuted the native inhabitants of England beyond all reason. Whether nobles or commons, I cruelly oppressed them; many I unjustly disinherited; innumerable multitudes, especially in the county of York, perished through me by famine and sword... I am stained with the rivers of blood that I have shed.*

THE DOMESDAY BOOK

The Domesday Book could easily have been called *1086: Who Owns What, How Much, When and Where.* William I needed to raise taxes to pay for his army and commissioned a thorough national survey to assess the wealth and assets of his subjects.

The first draft was completed in August 1086 and contained records for 13,418 settlements in the English counties south of the Rivers Ribble and Tees (the border with Scotland at the time). The finished report is 900 pages long and contains two million words. It can be seen today at the National Archives at Kew.

The *Anglo-Saxon Chronicle* reports that the inquiry was carried out so very thoroughly 'that there was not a single "hide", not one virgate of land, not even one ox, nor one cow, nor one pig that was not set down in his writ. And all the recorded particulars were afterwards brought to him.'

Richard Fitzneal, Henry II's Lord Treasurer, explained the Domesday reference in 1179:

> The book is metaphorically called by the native English Domesday, i.e. the Day of Judgement, for as the sentence of that strict and terrible last account cannot be evaded by any skilful subterfuge, so when this book is appealed to... its sentence cannot be quashed or set aside with impunity. That is why we have called the book

> 'the Book of Judgement'... because its decisions, like those of the Last Judgement, are unalterable.
>
> It was to be a work of reference for tax purposes and highlighted the immense changes that had taken place in land ownership. It clearly showed the ruthlessness of the Norman takeover – the old English ruling class had almost disappeared, with barely 5 per cent of land left in Saxon hands, to be replaced by 200 Norman barons and bishops as the new land-owning classes.

⚜ WILLIAM'S STICKY END

William's later years were not happy ones. His brother was in revolt and he was constantly at war. On one of his many incursions into France, King Philip had taunted him for being obese. A furious William ordered his troops to burn down the town of Mantes, 30 miles west of Paris, but as they looted and pillaged, his horse stood on a cinder and reared up, throwing the corpulent 60-year-old king forward in his saddle, causing serious internal injuries.

He was taken back to Rouen but died six weeks later. When the time came to bury the heavy body at Caen, it was discovered that the sarcophagus was not big enough. Orderic Vitalis reported that the bloated corpse was forced in: 'The swollen bowels burst, and an intolerable stench assailed the nostrils of the bystanders and the whole crowd.'

It was an ignominious end.

WILLIAM II (WILLIAM RUFUS)

1056–1100, reigned 1087–1100
Son of William I and
Matilda of Flanders

William II was the third son of William the Conqueror and could count himself fortunate to take the throne. The conqueror's eldest son, Robert Curthose, so-called because of the shortness of his legs and therefore his leggings, was made the Duke of Normandy and the second son, Richard, had been killed in a hunting accident, but William I chose his favourite, Rufus (so-called because of his ginger hair and ruddy complexion), to be King of England.

Robert's claim was a legitimate one and Rufus's journey to London from Rouen after his father died needed to be rapid. It was – and he was crowned two weeks later.

But it was not a happy reign: the chapter headings in a potted history could be Rebellions, Skirmishes, Deceit, Broken Promises and Savage Violence. Mutilations were common punishments. One nobleman, William of Eu, accused of treason, had his eyes pulled out and his testicles cut off on Rufus's orders.

BROTHERLY LOVE

There was no love lost between William and his eldest brother, Robert. Orderic Vitalis describes an incident that took place at L'Aigle in Normandy in 1078: 'William and his younger brother Henry, having grown bored with casting dice, decided to make mischief by emptying a chamber pot onto their brother Robert from an upper gallery, thus infuriating and shaming him. A brawl broke out, and their father had to intercede to restore order.'

 WILLIAM THE HERETIC

William II was an unpopular king, particularly with the church. He rejected Christianity, and when church positions fell vacant, he refused to fill them and pocketed the money. By the time of his death, he claimed the revenues of three bishoprics and a dozen abbeys.

Few people spoke well of him, either during his reign or after. His reputation suffered because he was a homosexual and an irreligious man in an age when prejudices were strong. According to his critics, he was addicted to every kind of vice, particularly 'lust and especially sodomy'. Male fashions under Rufus became extravagant and lavish, much to the disgust of disapproving churchmen.

The *Anglo-Saxon Chronicle* has strong views about William II:

In his days therefore, righteousness declined and every evil of every kind towards God and man put up its head. Everything that was hateful to God and to righteous men was the daily practice in this land during his reign. Therefore he was hated by almost all his people and abhorrent to God.

On the plus side, he did start to build what were two of the biggest buildings in Europe at that time: Westminster Hall (1097–1099) and Durham Cathedral.

⚜ A FAMOUS HUNTING ACCIDENT

In 1100, while hunting in the New Forest, William was killed by an arrow. Nobody knows whether it was an accident or murder. All his hunting friends curiously disappeared. He was found by a forest worker who took the body, with the arrow still sticking out, in a cart to Winchester. William's younger brother Henry was out hunting with him at the time of the accident/murder and this got the conspiracy theorists working over-time, especially as Henry made no effort to tend to his brother and coldly left the body by the roadside and galloped to Winchester to put in a claim for the crown.

The monks were terrified to see the king's body when it arrived in the cart and buried it as quickly as they could under one of the towers in the early hours of the morning. The tower fell down some years later. For the people, this clearly was the judgment of God, angry that a wicked man like William II had been buried there.

Contemporary accounts said William's death had been an accident, but later scholars suggested murder. Hunting accidents were common, and an inscription on the Rufus Stone, close to the A31 near Lyndhurst in Hampshire, says the arrow ricocheted off a tree before killing the king.

HENRY I (HENRY BEAUCLERC)

1068–1135, reigned 1100–1135
Son of William the Conqueror
and Matilda of Flanders

When William II died hunting in 1100, the throne should have passed to his elder brother Robert, Duke of Normandy. Henry was well aware of this and made a 60-mile dash to London and had himself crowned Henry I three days later, at the age of 31. Robert was away on a crusade; he had been away for four years and was on his way home when Henry took the throne.

Within three months Henry I had married Matilda of Scotland, who was descended from Alfred the Great and was the great-granddaughter of Edmund II. The marriage pleased the Scots and the Saxon English, and Henry consolidated his power, re-establishing the laws of his father, repealing William II's laws and recalling Anselm as Archbishop of Canterbury from France where he had been hiding from Rufus.

A response from Robert was inevitable and Henry's brother landed in England in 1101, but a peace was negotiated at Alton in Hampshire. Robert returned to Normandy but in 1106, Henry invaded Normandy to deal with some particularly troublesome barons. He captured Robert at Tinchebrai and imprisoned him for the rest of his life, 28 years. Robert spent his final years incarcerated in Cardiff Castle, being forced to learn Welsh. It is not clear which was the worse punishment.

Henry I was now Duke of Normandy as well as King of England, just like his father, William the Conqueror.

He had four legitimate heirs from his first marriage – but separately claimed the royal record for fathering illegitimate children: in fact, it seems they could not be bothered recording them any longer once the total had reached 25 – nine sons and 16 daughters.

⚜ THE WHITE SHIP

Henry had one legitimate son and heir, Prince William, but in a cruel and ironic twist of fate, he died in 1120, leaving England with no male heir. The king and his beloved son were in Normandy together, about to return to England.

A captain of the fleet approached the king to say that his father had steered *The White Ship*, which William the Conqueror had sailed in to England.

'Would you do me the honour of sailing in my boat?' the captain asked. The king said. 'No, but you may steer my son.'

The 300 passengers spent the day drinking and feasting, with more drinking on board. Eventually the boat set off. It skimmed over the waves like a beautiful bird, just as the captain said it would. Until, that is, it hit a rock not far out from Barfleur and the boat went crashing down with half the Anglo-Norman nobility on board. There was one survivor.

CHECKING ACCOUNTS

Henry I was very careful with money and he left a real and lasting financial legacy. In 1106 he introduced the Exchequer as a new way of government accounting and monitoring state income and expenditure. The Exchequer was a piece of chequered cloth laid out on a table about 10 feet by 5 feet and counters would be piled up on the different squares and counted. Twice a year, on Lady Day and at Michaelmas, officials had to bring in their money and have it checked and counted. We still have a Chancellor of the Exchequer, and also – for the time being at least – cheques.

Henry's firm grip on the economy also extended to the money supply. In 1124, at the Assize of the Moneyers, 94 moneyers (authorised coin minters) were found guilty of debasing the coin and were castrated and their right hands cut off. This is called keeping a very tight control of the supply of money – the very opposite of quantitative easing.

No one dared tell the king of the tragedy – he loved his son above everything. After a few days, one of the nobles' children was pushed into the king's room and told to say what had happened. The king was distraught – it is said that he never smiled again.

Henry, the 24th great-grandfather to Elizabeth II, died at Rouen from food poisoning after eating, famously, a 'surfeit of lampreys' in 1135. Lampreys are eel-like creatures that often contain toxins, and Henry had eaten too many of them. It took a week for him die, which at least gave him time to organise his funeral at Reading Abbey.

WHAT'S IN A NAME?

Henry was given the nickname Beauclerc by later historians, in an allusion to his great learning and scholarship.

STEPHEN

*c.*1097–1154, reigned 1135–1154
Son of Stephen, Count of Bois,
and Adela, daughter of William I

After the death of Prince William in 1125 on *The White Ship*, Henry I promised the throne to his daughter Matilda, who was married to Henry V, the Holy Roman Emperor and King of Germany.

The emperor died in 1125 and Henry I arranged a marriage for Matilda in 1128 to Geoffrey IV (the Handsome), Count of Anjou, who was 14 at the time. (He became handsome later.)

This was a move full of danger: the Anglo-Norman barons were completely against giving their allegiance to a woman, and certainly not one married to a member of the House of Anjou, sworn enemies of the House of Normandy.

But Henry's nephew, Stephen, a grandson of William the Conqueror, and one of the richest of the Anglo-French nobles, had a good claim to the throne. Despite having sworn allegiance to Matilda, he raced to London when Henry died to have himself crowned in December 1135.

Once he was King of England, the lords felt there was little they could do about it. The barons approved of him – he was mild, gentle and likeable, but these were not the characteristics needed for the next monarch.

Matilda was furious that Stephen had moved in to have himself crowned. She was a formidable opponent and commanded enough support to throw England into many years of turmoil. Matilda and her forces landed in Britain to fight him – this was the start of an extremely bitter and brutal civil war called the Anarchy that lasted all of Stephen's reign – almost 20 years.

For eight months, from February 1141, when Stephen was captured by Matilda's forces, until November of that year, she effectively became the first Queen of England, having the title Domina or Lady of the English. However, despite her achievement, she was never crowned.

66 ·

And so it went on for 19 years while
Stephen was king [...] the land was
laid waste: wherever the ground was tilled,
the earth produced no corn, because
the land was ruined by such doings.
And people said openly that Christ
and his saints were asleep.

A CONTEMPORANEOUS ENTRY
ON THE ANARCHY IN THE
ANGLO-SAXON CHRONICLE.

· ·

There was a constant struggle between the two factions but a deal between them was done when Stephen's heir, Eustace, died in 1153. It was agreed that King Stephen would keep the throne for his lifetime (which turned out in the end to be a very short time – he died the following year, in 1154), and would be succeeded by Matilda's son Henry. It was probably a relief all round that the succession should be settled on Matilda's son, rather than Matilda herself.

Matilda was unpopular but she did leave a lasting legacy – she was the mother of the Plantagenets, a royal house that would rule England for more than 300 years.

HOUSE OF PLANTAGENET

HENRY II

1139–1189, reigned 1154–1189
Son of Geoffrey IV, Count of Anjou,
and Matilda, daughter of Henry I

When Henry became King of England aged 21, after the death of Stephen, he was already Duke of Normandy, Count of Anjou and Duke of Aquitaine and head of the largest empire in Europe. This stretched from the Scottish borders to the south of France, an area greater than any other English king had ruled before him. In fact, he controlled more land in France than did the French King Louis VII. The empire remained intact until his death in 1189.

Henry was the most powerful monarch in Europe and vowed to keep it that way. He took the name Plantagenet after the sprig of bright-yellow common broom (*Planta genista*) that his father Geoffrey IV, Count of Anjou, wore on his black war helmet.

He was constantly on the move, spending 60 per cent of his reign abroad. And he insisted that his horses were always kept ready for him at abbeys around the country for one of his flying visits – Louis VII once said of Henry, 'Now in England, now in Normandy, he must fly rather than travel by horse or ship.'

With his thick-set frame and red hair, he was an impressive individual. 'His countenance,' said Walter Map, a royal chronicler, 'was one on which a man might gaze a thousand times yet still feel drawn to gaze again.'

This description was clearly accurate, because on a visit to France in 1151, when the French King Louis VII's wife, Eleanor, Duchess of Aquitaine, the greatest heiress in Europe, set eyes on Henry the result was quite extraordinary – she was infatuated. Eleanor was very beautiful and very rich. She demanded an annulment of her marriage and in the following year married Henry, ten years her junior, at Poitiers Cathedral. They would go on to have eight children together. Two years after their marriage in 1152, they were crowned in magnificent style in Westminster Abbey.

Henry was an outstanding king, and brought order to an England ravaged by civil war. He has been described as the greatest king England ever had.

 ## WHO WILL RID ME OF THIS MEDDLESOME PRIEST?

In his youth, Henry had been very friendly with the young Thomas Becket and he made him Chancellor in

1155, one year after becoming king. But everything changed when Henry made Becket Archbishop of Canterbury in 1162. From then on, the churchman became a changed man, eating only simple food and wearing simple and coarse clothes.

In 1164, Henry attempted to reassert his rights over the church. The Constitutions of Clarendon placed limits on the church's jurisdiction: the King said the church was subject to the law of the land. Becket refused to sign, saying the church was above the law. (Many of the reforms of the Assizes of Clarendon two years later made a lasting mark on legal procedure as we know it, such as the establishment of trial by a jury of 12.)

Both Becket and the Pope refused to approve the Constitutions and after a fierce argument, Becket sailed to exile in France. In 1170, Pope Alexander III threatened England with an interdict and Henry and Becket quarrelled again.

Becket returned to Canterbury from exile. The news threw King Henry into a rage in which he uttered words that were interpreted by his knights to mean that he wanted Becket killed. An eyewitness reported that the King shouted, 'What miserable drones and traitors have I nourished and brought up in my household, who let their lord be treated with such shameful contempt by a low-born cleric?'

The King's words have gone down in history as 'Who will rid me of this meddlesome priest?' or 'Will no one rid me of this troublesome priest?' Henry may have thought that, but he never said it exactly like that.

However he phrased his request, he was not short of volunteers. Four of Henry's knights rode to Canterbury and murdered Becket on 29 December 1170 before the high altar, cracking open his skull.

The effect was momentous. Henry realised that Becket had won – he was a martyr and very soon a saint, the victim of a monstrous murder in his own cathedral.

In a painful act of penitence, Henry walked barefoot into Canterbury wearing nothing but a hair shirt. In the cathedral he submitted to being beaten – three strokes from each of the 80 monks and five strokes from the bishops and abbots.

He then spent the next night in the cathedral crypt fasting and praying.

Despite this setback and humiliation, the King's hold on his empire did not seem to be affected by the Becket affair. He was at the height of his powers, but his personal life was to peter out and end sadly after he fell out with his wife, Eleanor.

Their passionate relationship had soured, the Queen understandably resentful of his promiscuity – particularly with Rosamund Clifford, known as the Fair Rosamund. Henry imprisoned Eleanor from 1173 until his death in 1189 and she was 67 when she was released.

His sons Richard and John, greatly encouraged by their mother, led a revolt against him. He was forced to agree to a humiliating peace with Philip II of France and was reported to have been extremely upset when, later in life, he learned that his favourite son, John, was one of the plotters. Henry died two days later at Chinon.

RICHARD I (RICHARD THE LIONHEART)

1157–1199, reigned 1189–1199
Son of Henry II and
Eleanor of Aquitaine

Richard spent less than six months in England during his ten-year reign. For most of the time, he was on one of his many military adventures. Encouraged by his mother, Eleanor, he was only 16 when he first campaigned with his brothers against his father, Henry II.

Richard was tall and handsome, a romantic as well as being a fearless warrior. His reputation as a soldier was based on his logistical skills as much as his bravery: for one crusade, he arranged for 60,000 horseshoes to be made and transported to the Middle East. Unfortunately, he has been judged to be a terrible king.

The Crusades started in 1095 when Pope Urban II urged Europe's knights to drive the Muslims out of the Holy Land and Jerusalem. The response to the Pope's appeal was enormous. One group of Crusaders captured Jerusalem in 1099 but it was retaken by the Salah-al-Din (Saladin), and in 1187, Pope Gregory VIII called for another Crusade to recapture the city.

Richard swore to 'take the Cross', to join the Crusade, and headed off for Jerusalem. Eleanor, his mother, turned up while Richard was on the way to the Holy Land with a bride for him, Berengaria of Navarre. Berengaria's ship was almost seized by the Greek ruler of Cyprus and Richard responded by invading and capturing the whole island. Richard and Berengaria married in Limassol in 1191 and Berengaria was crowned Queen of England and Cyprus.

Hers was a sad life. She was a beauty and seemed a good match for the handsome Richard, the most popular king in Christendom. She retired to France and was 34 when Richard died without an heir. She spent the rest of her life in a nunnery helping poor and abandoned children. In 1229, she built a beautiful abbey at l'Epau near Le Mans.

In 1191, Richard landed at Acre where the Crusaders had besieged the port for more than two years. Within five weeks of Richard's arrival, the port had fallen. Unhappy with the progress of talks after the end of the siege, he paraded 2,700 hostages through the town and had them slaughtered.

Richard became a Crusader hero but he never got closer than 12 miles from Jerusalem and a truce was struck: Jerusalem would remain in Muslim hands, but Christian pilgrims would be able to visit.

But then Richard received news from England in 1192 that his younger brother John had started a revolt against him. And so he had to race home. The journey home was disastrous. First, he was shipwrecked. Then he was captured near Vienna by Leopold V, Duke of Austria, who imprisoned him at Schloss Durnstein high above the Danube. The next year, Richard was taken to the Holy Roman Emperor Henry VI's castle at Trifels, where a massive ransom demand was made.

DID YOU KNOW?

The phrase *Dieu et mon droit* (God and My Right) was first used by Richard I as a battle cry. It would not have been strange for Richard to choose a French motto for his battle cry – after all, despite being born in Oxford, his first language was French and he hardly spoke a word of English.

The words were later picked up by Henry V and became the motto of the British monarchy.

 ## COEUR DE LION

Richard's cognomen of Lionheart or Coeur de Lion is generally thought to have referred to his bravery, but another quite incredible story from a Middle English romance gives an alternative reason for the nickname.

The incident was said to have occurred after Richard had had an affair with the daughter of a German king. The king imprisoned Richard and having starved a lion for a few days in his private zoo, put it in Richard's cell.

According to the story, Richard managed to borrow 40 silk handkerchiefs from his lover, wrapped them round his hands and after a fight with the lion, put his arm down the throat of the animal and pulled out its beating heart.

He then confronted the German king. According to a manuscript at Gonville and Caius College, Cambridge, Richard 'promptly exits his cell, carries the heart into the great hall and, in front of the entire court, rubs it in the table salt and eats it raw'.

Full marks to the romance writers of the day for piling incredulity on incredulity. But who knows, it might be true.

A MUSICAL LEGEND

Another legend has it that a wandering minstrel called Blondel, who had written poems and songs with Richard, went from castle to castle in Austria to try to find his master. Wherever Blondel travelled, he sang a song which Richard and he had sung together. Eventually one night he was singing beneath the castle walls when another voice took up the tune for the second verse from a window above him. It was Richard, and Blondel raced back to England with the joyous news. It is a gentle folk story but alas it does not stack up. Blondel had no need to go from castle to castle to find his liege – it was well known that Richard was imprisoned at Durnstein.

Eleanor and John between them managed to raise the ransom for King Richard's return – a true king's ransom. It is said that it was the equivalent of three times the annual income of the Crown. (Times have clearly changed – HMRC receipts for the UK for 2014 were £500bn). All the population was expected to contribute. The people of England suffered for years: there was a 25 per cent tax on income and the Cistercian sheep farms in England had to give a year's wool crop to the monarch.

Richard returned to England in 1194 before returning to France to reclaim the territories he had lost during his captivity. During a siege in France in 1199 he was hit in the shoulder by a stray arrow while inspecting his military fortifications. Gangrene set in and he died soon after.

The verdict on Richard I's reign was mixed: he played a very small part in the affairs of England but an important part in the affairs of Europe.

 A UNIQUE HONOUR

Richard I is the only monarch honoured with a statue outside the Houses of Parliament. Designed by French sculptor Baron Marochetti, a clay model was put on show at the Great Exhibition in 1851 and the magnificent statue was adjudged to be so good that it was cast in bronze and put in its present position in Old Palace Yard outside the House of Lords in 1860.

JOHN

1167–1216, reigned 1199–1216
Son of Henry II and Eleanor
of Aquitaine

For centuries, historians have agreed that King John was bad and duly rolled out all the adjectives to describe a bad king: cruel, incompetent, treacherous, seriously lecherous, untrustworthy, greedy, power-mad. History has indeed judged him to have been all those things – a bad king and a bad human being.

John was the youngest of the eight children of Henry II and Eleanor of Aquitaine, who was 45 when she gave birth to him. His parents became estranged, his mother effectively being put under house arrest in Winchester for 16 years, after which his brothers treated him shabbily. His father was not much better: as he had no territory to his name, his father nicknamed him Jean Sans Terre – John Lackland.

He married an heiress, Isabella of Gloucester, in 1189, but this marriage was annulled after he fell in love with another Isabella, this one of Angouleme, who was 12. They had six children and he fathered 12 illegitimate children with other women. He was a cruel man. Once when he thought his wife was having an affair, he had the man killed and the body hung over her bed.

John's sexual appetite knew no bounds and he viewed his barons' wives and daughters as fair game. On one occasion, he told Baron Eustace de Vesci that he was going to have sex with the baron's wife, Margaret. De Vesci quickly smuggled a prostitute into the marital bed. The following morning, John complimented him on his wife's performance.

His brother Richard had made John his successor, but a young nephew called Arthur was possibly closer in line to the throne. Arthur disappeared in sinister and suspicious circumstances to be found at the bottom of the River Seine with a stone tied to his body. It is hard not to believe that John did not have some hand in this.

John succeeded to the throne in 1199 and quarrelled with everyone throughout his reign: he lost most of his territory in France and by 1206, all English-held land north of the Loire had been lost. After John refused to appoint Stephen Langton, Pope Innocent III's candidate as Archbishop of Canterbury, the Pope imposed a papal interdict: all church services were banned from 1208 to 1214. The Pope excommunicated John from 1209 to 1213.

High taxation had upset the barons who were in open rebellion and in 1215 they forced him to sign (or more accurately, to affix his seal to) the Magna Carta, the Great Charter – one of the most celebrated documents in history. It was the most important legacy that came out of his reign.

ENGLAND'S GREAT CHARTER: THE MAGNA CARTA

The Magna Carta, signed at Runnymede on the Thames near Egham, imposed limits on the king's power and guaranteed some rights for the barons in government. It established for the first time the principle that no man – not even the king – was above the law of the land. It remains a cornerstone of the British constitution, and constitutions around the world.

There were 63 clauses. The 39th clause gave all free men the right to justice and a fair trial:

> No free man shall be seized or imprisoned, or stripped of his rights or possessions, or outlawed or exiled, or deprived of his standing in any other way, nor will we proceed with force against him, or send others to do so, except by the lawful judgement of his equals or by the law of the land.

Clause 40 was also a fundamental principle:

> To no one will we sell, to no one deny, or delay right or justice.

The charter was a peace treaty effectively imposed on the King by the barons and provided a new framework for the relationship between the King and his subjects. The charter was reissued in 1216, 1217, 1225 and then in 1297.

The sentiments of Magna Carta have echoed down the ages, and although many of the clauses were short-lived, the key principle of the rule of law and due process has become a cornerstone for democracies everywhere.

Magna Carta played an important part in the American Revolution: one-third of the clauses of the American Bill of Rights in 1791 come straight from Magna Carta. Although only three of the document's clauses are relevant in Britain today, 17 of America's 50 states include Magna Carta in full on their statute books.

There are four known surviving versions of the 1215 Magna Carta: two are in the British Library in London, one in Lincoln Cathedral and one in Salisbury Cathedral. All were put on display in 2015 for the 800th anniversary.

⚜ LOST TREASURE

Towards the end of his reign, John grew increasingly unpopular and increasingly paranoid about security, and he began taking the Crown Jewels with him wherever he went. On 12 October 1216, he attempted to cross the Wash (a large bay that separates East Anglia from Lincolnshire) as he moved north with his royal baggage train to try to get to Lincolnshire.

He took the longer route by way of Wisbech and sent the baggage train, which included the Crown Jewels, on a shortcut along a causeway and through a ford across the mouth of the river. This route was useable only at low tide, but the horse-drawn wagons moved too slowly for the incoming tide, and many were lost.

John organised a search for the baggage train, but it was never found. In the disaster he lost all his treasure: the crown of Edward the Confessor, Matilda's crown, the orb and sceptre and all the jewellery of his mother, Eleanor of Aquitaine, once the richest woman in the world.

The loss of the treasure and the more prosaic, everyday items such as gold cups and chalices meant that the King had become powerless. Within days, he caught a fever that led to dysentery and he died soon after at Newark aged 48. He was buried in Worcester Cathedral.

It may not be the fairest of epitaphs but certainly it is one of the most direct: Matthew Paris was moved to write, 20 years after his death: 'Foul as it is, hell itself is defiled by the foulness of King John.'

HENRY III

1207–1272, reigned 1216–1272
Son of John and Isabella
of Angouleme

Henry was nine when he was crowned just ten days after his father died and he was to reign for 56 years. One description of him at his coronation at Gloucester Cathedral goes: 'This tiny spark of minute beauty, the sole hope for the torn kingdom.' It must have been a moving scene.

In 1220, Henry was re-crowned at Westminster Abbey – this time with all the pomp and ceremony that was fitting. He still was only 13.

Henry took over the reins in 1227, but was not popular with the barons, whom he alienated by giving favours to a seemingly never-ending influx of French relations and advisors, especially after his marriage to Eleanor of Provence in 1236. Her family demanded that they were given positions at the English court and bishoprics. For the English barons it was déjà vu, just like the days of Edward the Confessor and William the Conqueror again.

Henry broke the Magna Carta ten times and made an error of judgment when he sacked Simon de Montfort, his brother-in-law, as Governor of Gascony. De Montfort was to become the leader of the barons against the king.

In 1258, the lords demanded that Henry should call a Great Council of lords and bishops to assist the king on all important matters. Henry was forced to accept the Provisions of Oxford, in effect a council limiting the power of the king.

In 1261, Henry repealed the Provisions with the help of the Pope, and battle lines were drawn for armed conflict. De Montfort won the first round of this civil war at the Battle of Lewes in 1264.

Henry III was captured and imprisoned and de Montfort took over, summoning a Great Council that included two citizens from each city and two knights from each shire, as well as all the lords and bishops. This was the first time non-nobles had been involved in government and was the precursor of the House of Commons. It met at Kenilworth in 1265.

Henry's son Edward came to his father's rescue after the Battle of Lewes. He raised an army in East Wales and was victorious at the Battle of Evesham in 1265.

After Evesham, Henry regained his throne and Edward took on more responsibility, allowing Henry to indulge his interests in architecture and the arts.

In the 1220s, Henry spent much of his time starting to extend and expand Westminster Abbey, one reason for which was that he wanted to rebuild the shrine for his hero, Edward the

Confessor. It was finished in 1289. Ecclesiastical architecture enjoyed a golden age thanks in no small part to the influence of French architects and craftsmen who came over to England.

It was in Henry III's time that Early English Gothic architecture took hold and his reign saw work on some of the most beautiful cathedrals in that style: the magnificent West Front at Wells was completed in 1250, and the jewel in the crown, Salisbury Cathedral, was finished in 1258.

WEDDING PRESENT: OPEN WITH CARE

Towards the end of King John's reign a zoo was established at the Tower of London, with a polar bear that swam in the Thames on a tether, lions, snakes, a rhinoceros and an elephant. The polar bear was a gift to Henry III from Haakon IV of Norway and in 1236, the Holy Roman Emperor Frederick II sent Henry three lions as a wedding gift when he married the Emperor's sister. The Royal Arms of England has featured three lions passant since Richard I's time and the three lions still adorn the England football team's shirt. Admission to the menagerie was limited but free; later visitors had to pay, or bring a cat or dog as food for the animals.

EDWARD I

1239–1307, reigned 1272–1307
Son of Henry III and
Eleanor of Provence

Edward was named by his father Henry III in honour of his favourite saint, Edward the Confessor. In 1254, at the age of 15, he married his 13-year-old cousin Eleanor of Castile and was given land in Gascony previously in the hands of Simon de Montfort.

Even though the marriage was clearly an arranged political alliance, for Edward and Eleanor it was seemingly a happy one – they had 16 children together.

Prince Edward's first chance to show off his military skills had come at the Battle of Evesham in 1265. This was a bloody battle: 4,000 rebel troops were killed in what was a massacre. A contemporary chronicler Arnald FitzThedmar said De Montfort himself was killed by Roger Mortimer, leader of the King's forces, and dismembered, his head severed from his body, and his testicles cut off and hung on either side of his nose, in the style of the day. In this state, Mortimer sent the head to his arch-royalist wife, Lady Maud, at Wigmore Castle as a treasured gift.

Edward was king in all but name now as his father grew older. He went on a crusade with 1,000 men and at one time captured Nazareth.

En route back to England, news came that Henry III had died and that Edward was king in his own right. He landed at Dover after being away for four years to receive a rapturous reception.

A FEAST TO REMEMBER

The coronation celebrations in 1274 went on for two weeks: 380 cattle, 430 sheep, 450 pigs, 18 wild boars, 278 flitches of bacon and 20,000 fowls were used for the feast.

THE BATTLE FOR WALES

Edward soon had to deal with Wales: Marcher Lords managed to keep the peace in the south and central parts of the country, but in the north, the Gwynedd princes refused to submit to English rule.

Llywelyn ap Gruffudd declared himself Prince of Wales and went about expanding his lands and refused to pay homage to Edward six times, before the king lost his patience.

Edward's response was to mobilise, at Worcester in 1277, one of the biggest armies ever seen in Britain –1,000 knights in armour, and around 15,000 foot solders. The army marched up the Severn and Dee Valleys north to the mouth of the River Conwy.

Anglesey was quickly taken and, surrounded and threatened with starvation in his castle in Snowdonia, Llywelyn sued for peace. Llywelyn's brother Dafydd led a new rebellion in 1282, and Llywelyn was killed in battle at Cilmeri, Powys; his head was cut off and taken to London and carried through the streets on a spear to the Tower of London.

Edward decided that building castles was the answer to keeping the Welsh in line. He found a builder of genius in James of St George and today the castles at Conwy, Harlech, Rhuddlan, Beaumaris and Caernarfon are a testimony to their vision and beauty as well as a physical expression of the brute power of the king. The Statute of Rhuddlan in 1284 effectively annexed Wales to the English crown, with English laws and government administration being introduced.

 THE ELEANOR CROSSES

Edward I's wife Eleanor died in 1290. The King, who normally showed little emotion, was deeply affected and had a memorial cross erected at every place where her body had rested during the journey back to London from Lincoln. There were 12 of them and they were known as the Eleanor Crosses. Only three are still standing – at Geddington and Hardingstone, both in Northamptonshire, and Waltham Cross, Essex. Charing Cross was the last stage of the journey and the cross there today in front of the railway station is a replica after the original was destroyed in the Civil War in 1647. It was originally sited where the statue of Charles I stands at the top of Whitehall. Eleanor has been graced with a magnificent gilt-bronze effigy by William Torel in Westminster Abbey. Gold florins were brought from Italy for the gilding.

⚜ LONGSHANKS VS BRAVEHEART

In 1299, when he was 60, Edward married Margaret, the daughter of King Philip III of France. She was 17 and they had three children.

Edward I respected the Magna Carta and regularly consulted the Great Council. In 1295 he summoned the biggest council yet, made up of barons, bishops, knights and burgesses – it became known later as the Model Parliament – England's first parliament.

He then turned his attention to Scotland where there were 13 claimants for the vacant Scottish throne. Edward invaded Scotland and in 1296 besieged Berwick, whose citizens mocked the King, who was 6 feet 2 inches with long thin legs, calling him 'Longshanks'. Not a good move.

On his long-time favourite warhorse, Bayard, a furious Edward led the assault on the town and vaulted a ditch and a palisade ending up in the centre of the town. English troops followed him into the narrow streets and fighting gave way to a general massacre.

Upwards of 15,000 people were killed. Tales of brutality abounded: women and children being put to the sword; thousands being hanged; buildings burned with those inside perishing in the flames. The bloodshed lasted three days while every hiding place was searched and all those found were slaughtered.

In an extremely provocative move, the Stone of Scone, the symbol of Scottish monarchy, on which Scottish kings were crowned was then taken to Westminster in 1296, where it stayed until 1996.

A Scottish knight, William Wallace, raised an army and defeated the English at Stirling Bridge in 1297. With his pride dented, Edward invaded Scotland again and the two armies met at Falkirk in 1298. To the Scots' surprise, archers from Wales came to the rescue of the English monarch for the first time, but not the last. Only Wallace and a handful of his men survived. Longshanks gained a new nickname at Falkirk – the Hammer of the Scots – which is etched on his simple tomb in Westminster Abbey. Wallace was eventually captured attempting to storm Stirling Castle in 1304. But the Scots refused to be cowed and Edward's plan to unite the two countries was unsuccessful.

 ## THE PRINCE OF WALES

In 1301, with Llywelyn now almost 20 years dead, Edward I appropriated the title of Prince of Wales. He conferred it on his son, Edward, at his new castle at Caernarfon where the future Edward II had been born. The title has been bestowed on all male heirs apparent to this day. Prince Charles is the 21st heir to hold the title.

EDWARD II

1284–1327, reigned 1307–1327
Son of Edward I and
Eleanor of Castile

Edward I died in July 1307 and, his three elder brothers having predeceased him, his son Edward became king. One of his first acts as king was to recall his favourite Piers Gaveston from exile.

Edward I had banished him to France for his bad influence on his son 'and the undue intimacy which the young Lord Edward had adopted towards him'. Gaveston was given the earldom of Cornwall by Edward II.

It was plain that Edward's sexual appetites were centred on the effete and vain Gaveston. Despite this, Edward married Isabella of France at Boulogne in 1308 and when she came to England, the 12-year-old queen soon noticed that Gaveston was wearing jewellery that her father had given to Edward as a wedding present. Isabella's family were reported to be so angered by the two men's behaviour at the wedding banquet that they walked out.

Later that year, Gaveston was exiled to France for his extravagance only to return the next year. Parliament set up a committee of Lords Ordainers – a committee of 21 earls, barons and bishops – in 1310 to try to control the king and regulate the royal household. Gaveston was exiled permanently and when he returned to court, he was kidnapped by the king's opponents and was hanged, drawn and quartered.

Edward's shortcomings as a military leader were highlighted at Bannockburn in 1314 when Robert Bruce, grandson of an earlier Robert Bruce, humiliated the English.

Bruce ambushed Edward's large army as it moved to relieve Stirling Castle, which was under siege. Two days of fighting ended in a famous victory for the Scots – Edward lost two-thirds of his men. The battle assured Scottish independence for another four centuries until the Act of Union in 1707 was to bind the two countries together.

Edward took up with the Welsh border barons le Despenser family, father and son, and both called Hugh.

Baronial disaffection spread and by 1322 there was open civil war. Edward led a campaign against the royal opposition, the Lords Ordainers were dissolved and any legislation limiting royal power was ignored.

In 1326, Isabella took a lover, Roger Mortimer, and led an invasion from France and seized power. The elder Despenser was hanged, drawn and quartered; the young Despenser suffered the same fate a month later.

In 1327, Edward II was formally deposed by Parliament in favour of Edward III and was murdered on his wife's orders. There are conflicting reports of how he died and where he died (and indeed more recently, whether he died at all). The most lurid, not necessarily the most accurate account, has him killed at Berkeley Castle in Gloucestershire by means of a red-hot poker shoved up his fundament.

It was said that Edward I's greatest disappointment was Edward II, and that Edward II's greatest achievement was Edward III.

 ### HANGED, DRAWN AND QUARTERED

The worst crime in the eyes of the state was treason, however defined, and merited the most barbaric punishment – to be hanged, drawn and quartered.

The man found guilty was tied to a hurdle or wooden panel, and drawn by a horse to the place of execution, to be hanged (almost to the point of death), then emasculated. A long incision would be made from the neck to the navel and his bowels extracted and burned on a fire in front of him, i.e. he would be 'drawn' like a chicken before cooking. Next he was beheaded and quartered, chopped into four pieces 'to be disposed of at the King's pleasure'.

EDWARD III

1312–1377, reigned 1327–1377
Son of Edward II and
Isabella of France

Edward III was energetic and effective in his youth, magnificent and majestic in middle age and sadly, frail and senile in old age. He outlived his successes.

He became king when he was 14 after his father was murdered by his mother, Isabella. Early in his reign he caught his mother and her lover, Roger Mortimer, in a bedroom at Nottingham Castle. Mortimer was executed in 1330 after a show trial and although his mother was pardoned, she was put under house arrest in Norfolk for the rest of her life.

Edward was now free to rule. The barons welcomed a monarch who showed all the qualities of a great medieval king and flocked to his cultured court.

He appeared to be a model Plantagenet male, loving wine, women and song, war and pageantry.

In 1328, Charles of France died and Edward claimed to be the rightful King of France through the line of his mother and he vowed to assert his claim against a rival claim by Charles's cousin Philip VI of Valois.

Money and men were raised for this purpose, and Parliament granted the essential taxes to pay for the campaigns. In 1337, he publically stated his intention to win the throne of France. The Hundred Years' War had begun.

The 'war', which lasted from 1337 to 1453 (116 years), describes a series of battles and campaigns in a long drawn-out power struggle between England and France in those years.

Edward won resounding victories over the French at sea. The Battle of Sluys off Flanders in 1340 gave him control of the English Channel, and he defeated the Scots first at Halidon Hill near Berwick, and then more decisively at Neville's Cross, Durham, in 1345.

Edward's first major incursion into France took him to the walls of Paris in 1346, where they were badly hit by that dreaded battlefield enemy – dysentery. He withdrew to the River Somme – an area later to become synonymous with violent battles – and won a famous victory at the Battle of Crécy in 1346 over a large French army.

It was at Crécy that the longbow was first used – with terrible effects for the French knights in armour. To use it required immense strength, but in the hands of the Welsh archers the longbow could fire ten arrows a minute compared with the French crossbow's two. It penetrated armour at 200 yards.

The French had the numerical advantage, but superior English battle tactics, and the longbow, won the day. Around 10,000 French soldiers are said to have been killed, compared to the loss of only 100 English troops.

BOHEMIAN FEATHERS AND GERMAN WORDS

The King of Bohemia died in the battle of Crécy and legend has it that Edward's 16-year-old son, Edward of Woodstock, the future Black Prince, took Bohemia's three ostrich feathers as his crest along with the German motto *Ich dien* (I Serve). The heir to the English throne, the Prince of Wales, has held both the crest and the motto ever since.

It is not clear how Edward the Prince of Wales got the name the Black Prince. It was a name that was not used until 150 years after he died.

It is thought it refers to his black shield with the three ostrich feathers that he called his peace shield – it probably was used for jousting. It could also have referred to his black armour. He was known to wear a black surcoat over his armour in battle and his horse's caparison was black too.

It has also been said that that it was Edward's pride in his Welsh archers that led him to choose *Ich dien* as his motto. *Ich dien* is a very close homophone for the Welsh phrase *Eich dyn* (Your Man) and there were newspaper reports in 1917, when the Royal House of Saxe-Coburg and Gotha changed its name to Windsor to sound less German, that the Prince of Wales's motto might be changed from the German to the Welsh.

Correspondence was sent to Prime Minister David Lloyd George and the College of Heralds looked at the issue.

DID YOU KNOW?

So critical was the longbow to the English army that Edward banned all other sports, including football, on Sundays so his subjects could be free to concentrate on archery.

⚜ THE KNIGHTS OF THE GARTER

After their victory at Crécy, Edward's army then marched on Calais and besieged the town for several months before capturing it in 1347; it would remain in English hands for the best part of 200 years.

Froissart wrote that the king returned home in triumph: '*Le beau chevalier sans peur et sans reproche.*' He added: 'His like has not been seen since the days of King Arthur', a reference that Edward must have greatly enjoyed.

Inspired by Arthurian legends, Edward had wanted to establish a round table of knights and in 1348, he founded an order of chivalry, the Most Noble Order of the Garter, membership to which became the highest honour the monarch could confer. It was based, and still is, at St George's Chapel at Windsor.

The origin of this order lies in an incident that took place in Edward's court: one day, a garter slipped from the leg of a society beauty. The King put it on his own leg and remarked: '*Honi soit qui mal y pense*' – 'Shame be to him that thinks ill of it', which was probably directed against anyone who opposed the King's plan to win the French Crown. This is still the motto of the Knights of the Garter.

⚜ THE BLACK PRINCE

His son the Black Prince won the second great English victory over the French in the Hundred Years' War at Poitiers in 1356. There had been negotiations before the battle in which the Black Prince offered to hand over the booty from his recent military expeditions and to offer a seven-year truce. King Jean II of France turned down the offer because he was absolutely certain that the numerical supremacy of the French forces meant they were unbeatable.

The English had a force of 7,000 knights, men at war and archers and France mustered around 35,000 troops. In some ways, Poitiers was a more spectacular English victory than Crécy.

Jean was captured and brought to the Tower of London. Two foreign kings were now imprisoned there: the King of Scotland had been captured at Neville's Cross, and incarcerated. It is said that Edward treated the captured kings as honoured guests.

In 1360, with the Treaty of Bretigny, Edward was forced to renounce his claim to the French throne, although England still controlled a quarter of France. However, keeping control of such a vast amount of land proved to be impossible and under the Treaty of Bruges in 1375, France re-took all their land save for Calais and a small part of Gascony.

In 1369, his wife, Philippa of Hainault, died after 40 years of marriage – they had eight sons and five daughters – and Edward came under the malevolent influence of his mistress, Alice Perrers, with whom he had three illegitimate children.

The King himself, once the greatest warrior in Europe, became frail and prematurely senile and a victim of his mistress, who stole his jewels before she was banished in 1376 by the Good Parliament set up to stop growing royal corruption.

The heir to the throne, Edward the Black Prince, predeceased his father in 1376, dying of an illness contracted on one of his many foreign ventures. Edward III died just one year later, in 1377, and his effigy lies in Westminster Abbey.

 ## THE BLACK DEATH

The Black Death, which was almost certainly the disease we know today as bubonic plague, swept across Europe from around 1340 – some estimates say that as many as 25 million people may have died.

Between 1348 and 1350, it killed one and a half million people in England out of an estimated population of 4 million. It was to strike England another six times before the turn of the 15th century. First it devastated Bristol and then London, before continuing to East Anglia and the Midlands. Some estimates put the mortality rate as high as 50 per cent.

The first signs were a fever and black, foul-smelling boils. Victims usually died within 48 hours. Carried by rat fleas, the infection spread very quickly.

It was so virulent that one observer said that the 'living were scarce able to bury the dead'. It affected all of Europe.

RICHARD II

1367–1400, reigned 1377–1399
Son of the Edward, the Black Prince,
and Joan of Kent

The year before Edward III died, his son and heir Edward, the Black Prince, had died. Richard took the crown when he was aged ten and the kingdom was ruled at first by Richard's uncles John of Gaunt and Thomas of Gloucester.

Richard was a teenager and interested in clothes and fashion and all things artistic. He was not a warrior and paid much attention to two young courtiers, Robert de Vere, Marquis of Oxford, and Michael de la Pole, even after his marriage to Anne of Bohemia in 1382 when he was 15.

Thomas of Walsingham described the indolent courtiers as 'the Knights of Venus: more effective in the bedchamber than the field'.

But Richard did display real personal courage during the Peasants' Revolt in 1381 when he was only 14. The revolt was a demonstration against the poll tax imposed by John of Gaunt in which everybody, rich or poor, had to pay the same amount. This was universally hated, and riots broke out when the tax was being collected. It was the start of the Peasants' Revolt.

Wat Tyler, a craftsman from Kent, became the leader of the peasants and led a march on London to demand the King abolish peasants' obligations to their landlords. They went on the rampage when they reached London, burned down John of Gaunt's Savoy Palace on the Strand and murdered the Archbishop of Canterbury.

At Smithfield, a mob gathered and in the chaos, the Mayor of London stabbed and killed Tyler. Seeing this, Tyler's men leapt forward and ran towards the King with their bows ready to shoot. Richard boldly rode towards the rioters and said: 'What, sirs? Will you kill your king? I am your king. I will be your leader – follow me.'

The mob dispersed. It was Richard II's finest moment, certainly finer than when he later reneged on all the promises he had made to the peasants.

His court was flamboyant, and entertainment and lavish banquets were on a large scale, which led him to be described as 'the best… vyander of all Christian kings' in a cookery book published in 1390.

He completed the hammer-beam roof at Westminster Hall and ordered his own tomb in Westminster Abbey. It was a double effigy and it showed him holding hands with his wife, Anne, who died, aged 28 and childless, in 1394.

The country needed an heir, and in 1396 Richard married again – a seven-year-old French princess called Isabella. It seems a strange choice of wife for a king and a country needing an heir as quickly as possible.

Parliamentary power had become too established for Richard and in 1397 he tried to reintroduce absolute royal authority. But he had overreached himself.

He had exiled Henry Bolingbroke, who became Duke of Lancaster on the death of John of Gaunt, and seized his possessions.

This was the signal for Bolingbroke to return from exile and lead a rebellion; Richard was forced to surrender to his cousin; the King was made to abdicate and Bolingbroke became King Henry IV in 1399.

Richard II was imprisoned at Pontefract Castle in Yorkshire. A few months later, the patron of Chaucer (who finished *Canterbury Tales* in 1395), and the subject of *The Wilton Diptych*, an exquisitely beautiful painting finished in England in 1395, was dead, almost certainly of starvation.

HOUSE OF LANCASTER

HENRY IV

1367–1413, reigned 1399–1413
Son of John of Gaunt
and Blanche of Lancaster

Henry Bolingbroke was only a few months older than his cousin Richard II. His father John of Gaunt, Duke of Lancaster, was the third son of Edward III, and was so-called not for his physique but for the fact that he came from Ghent.

When John of Gaunt died in 1399, Richard II seized Henry's inheritance, the Duchy of Lancaster, the largest landholding in England. Bolingbroke had spent nine months in exile in France, but returned to Britain capturing Richard and imprisoning him.

Richard's rightful heir was Edmund Mortimer, 5th Earl of March, a direct descendant of Edward III's second son Lionel,

Duke of Clarence. But Edmund was a small boy and Henry managed to persuade Parliament that it would be better if he himself took the throne, which he did, at the age of 32.

The reign was a muddled and bad-tempered one, with rebellion after rebellion – Shakespeare described it as a scrambling and unquiet time.

In the late 14th century, Wycliffe had translated the Bible into English for the first time, an act of extreme courage, and one that brought him into direct conflict with the church in Rome. His Bible was widely distributed throughout England, and had a huge influence at the time, anticipating in some ways the Reformation.

In 1401, a statute on the burning of heretics led to many Lollards, followers of Wycliffe, being burned at the stake. The word Lollard comes from the Dutch word for 'mutterer'. In 1409, the Constitutions of Oxford made it heresy to translate the Bible into English.

Henry IV's troubles started soon after he took the throne. Owain Glyndwr led a revolt in Wales in 1401 that lasted ten years and then Henry had to withstand three rebellions by the Percy family from Northumberland, his former allies. He defeated them at the Battle of Shrewsbury in 1403 when Henry Percy (Harry Hotspur) was killed.

Henry IV is said to have wept when the body was taken to him, and when rumours started that he was still alive, the King exhumed the body; the head was impaled at York and the four quarters of the body were sent to London, Newcastle, Bristol and Chester. The victory at Shrewsbury did not stem the opposition and Henry had to repulse further revolts in 1405 and 1408.

In later life, worn down by conflict and financial problems and still suffering a guilt complex about the succession, he was afflicted by an illness similar to eczema that left him forever itching.

He hoped to make a crusade so that he could gain some forgiveness; a mystic predicted he would die in Jerusalem. He collapsed one day at prayer in Westminster Abbey and was taken to a nearby room. When he asked where he was, he was told the Jerusalem Chamber. Knowing that he had been told he would die in Jerusalem, he died soon after, an unhappy man, which was seen as divine retribution for the overthrow and murder of a king.

Shakespeare wrote a famous epitaph for him and his reign in *Henry IV, Part 2*, Act 3, scene 1, 26–31. The King complains that he can never relax and enjoy a good night's sleep like his countrymen; the speech ends with the famous line: 'Uneasy lies the head that wears a crown.'

HENRY V

1387–1422, reigned 1413–1422
Son of Henry IV and Mary de Bohun

Henry V is one of the best-known and best-loved English kings. Even without his PR man William Shakespeare, his victory at Agincourt would guarantee him a place in the pantheon.

He was born at Monmouth Castle, the son of Henry Bolingbroke. He accompanied his father on a number of military forays in his youth – he was 16 when he fought with valour at the Battle of Shrewsbury in 1403, where Harry Hotspur, who had once taught him, was killed.

Henry was crowned when he was 25 – it snowed that day in April 1413, and people were not sure whether this was a good omen or a bad one. Henry became a skilled tactician in matters both political and military.

Internal troubles in France gave him the chance to reassert his claims to the French throne inherited from the earlier Plantagenets. After two invasions, he restored England's empire in France for a short time.

⚜ THE BATTLE OF AGINCOURT

Henry set sail for Harfleur in Normandy in 1415 where he laid siege. After a month, the town surrendered but many troops contracted dysentery and around one-third of his army of 10,000 died.

A planned march on Paris was abandoned and he decided to head for Calais to sail home to England. But his depleted army ran into the French forces who were waiting for him in north-west France near Agincourt.

Historians are still debating what the difference was in the size of the two armies. Some say the English were outnumbered 2 to 1, others 3 to 1 and others 4 to 1 and more. Henry seemed to have had around 6,000 troops and France in excess of 20,000. One estimate has 8,000 English troops and 50,000 French. Either way, the English were heavily outnumbered.

The bedraggled English army settled down on the eve of the battle. They were weakened by sickness, and it rained all night, so that on the morning of 25 October 1415, St Crispin's Day, they were exhausted and sodden. The battleground was a not-very-large muddy field that was about to become a quagmire.

The French cavalry and armoured knights struggled in the mud and the English and Welsh longbowmen cut swathes through their lines. The archers used specially sharpened arrows made at the Tower of London. So many French soldiers were cut down that reinforcements from the back could not get through.

WE BAND OF BROTHERS

As imagined by Shakespeare, Henry V's speech to his troops before the battle has gone down as a classic motivational speech.

> From this day to the ending of the world,
> But we in it shall be remember'd;
> We few, we happy few, we band of brothers;
> For he to-day that sheds his blood with me
> Shall be my brother; be he ne'er so vile,
> This day shall gentle his condition;
> And gentlemen in England now-a-bed
> Shall think themselves accursed they were not here,
> And hold their manhoods cheap whiles any speaks
> That fought with us upon Saint Crispin's day.

Henry V, Act 4, scene 3, 58–67

The Battle of Agincourt was an overwhelming victory for Henry – 6,000 Frenchmen killed with English casualties less than 400.

The English and Welsh archers believed that the French intended to cut off the first and second fingers of the right hand of every captured archer to prevent him from again using a bow. The archers relished raising those two fingers to the advancing French as a gesture of defiance that the British still enjoy to this day.

Henry returned home to a hero's welcome: at Dover, he was carried shoulder high from his boat to the shore; villagers turned out in their thousands to greet him on his way to London; city worthies met him at Blackheath and escorted him to London Bridge, a journey that took five hours. It was joy unbounded.

A REQUEST THAT WAS HARD TO REFUSE

Money to help pay for the French campaigns was raised by loans rather than taxes. In May 1415, Henry sent letters appealing for money to individuals and to towns. A town would decide on the amount of the loan, and all citizens would then be assessed for a contribution.

One rich cloth merchant in London who lent money to Henry was Sir Richard Whittington, aka Dick Whittington. He was Lord Mayor of London three times. More of him later.

 KING OF FRANCE

In 1417–1418, he invaded France again and regained the Duchy of Normandy but it was five years after Agincourt before Henry could enter Paris. In the Treaty of Troyes 1420, the King of France, Charles the Mad, recognised Henry as his heir, and Henry married the King's daughter Catherine of Valois.

An English king was at last acknowledged as the King of England and France.

Ironically, Henry was the first medieval king who did not speak French.

Keeping hold of the English supremacy proved to be difficult and expensive as were efforts to gain even more territory in France. Tragedy struck in 1422, when Henry contracted dysentery. He died in Vincennes Castle aged 35.

Henry and his wife, Catherine, had recently had a son. He was ten months old and called Henry, but he was to be a very different king than his father.

HENRY VI

1421–1471, reigned 1422–1461;
1470–1471
Son of Henry V and Catherine
of Valois

Henry VI's long reign was as unsuccessful as the short reign of his father was memorable. He was nine months old when he became King of England and two months later, on the death of Charles VI, he became King of France. Humphrey, Duke of Gloucester, was appointed Regent of England and John, Duke of Bedford, Regent of France.

When he attended his first opening of Parliament, according to a report at the time, he 'shrieked and cried'. Well, he was three years old.

The Hundred Years' War was still rumbling on, and French pride was restored by Joan of Arc, a peasant girl from north-eastern France. In 1429, she claimed she had a vision from the Virgin Mary to drive the English out of France. Joan led a French army to Orleans to defeat the Anglo-Burgundians. Two years later, she was burned at the stake in Rouen as a witch and heretic. She was 19. Henry VI cannot be blamed for this – he was still only eight years old.

He took over in 1437 when he was 16 but it was another 16 years before the Hundred Years' War ended in 1453, 116 years after it started. The English had finally been driven out of France – Normandy was lost in 1450 and Gascony in 1451.

In 1454, Richard, Duke of York was made Protector after Henry had what today would be called a mental breakdown. A contemporary described him as 'unsteadfast of wit' and bouts of the illness left him in a catatonic state. York was dismissed as Protector a year later, heralding the start of the Wars of the Roses, in essence a family feud writ large. He went on to raise an army and defeated the Lancastrian forces at the Battle of St Albans in 1455, the first battle of the Wars of the Roses.

Most wars are driven by a principle of some sort – ideology, beliefs, national interest, religion, self-defence, even geography. The War of the Roses had none of the above – it was purely a struggle for power between two branches, Lancaster and York, of one family, the Plantagenets.

Richard, Duke of York, was the leader of the Yorkists; Henry VI's formidable wife, Margaret of Anjou, became the leader of the Lancastrians.

In 1461, Henry VI was deposed by Richard's son Edward, Duke of York, who was crowned Edward IV, after the Battle of Towton.

Henry VI regained, and then lost, his throne in a short-lived restoration in 1470. He was captured and taken to the Tower of London and died, presumed murdered, in 1471.

Henry was a pious man regarded by some as a saint and there still is a Henry VI Society trying to get him sanctified.

LILIES AND ROSES

A marble tablet in the Wakefield Tower at the Tower of London marks the spot where Henry VI is said to have met his untimely end. Each year, on the eve of the anniversary of his death, the Ceremony of the Lilies and the Roses is held: white lilies for Eton College and white roses for King's College, Cambridge, both institutions founded by Henry VI, are placed there in his memory.

HOUSE OF YORK

EDWARD IV

1442–1483, reigned 1461–1470;
1471–1483
Son of Richard, Duke of York,
and Cecily Neville

There were now two Kings of England – Henry VI, head of the House of Lancaster, and Edward IV, head of the House of York.

Richard, Duke of York, whose attempted coup in 1455 marked the start of the Wars of the Roses, was killed at the Battle of Wakefield in 1460. His son took the throne as Edward IV after the Yorkists won the Battle of Towton near Selby in Yorkshire in 1461. This was the bloodiest battle on English soil since Hastings, fought in the snow and one estimate is that up to 30,000 soldiers perished – one per cent of the total population. The little beck coursing through the bloodied battlefield was reported to have flowed deep red.

Edward IV held on to the throne until 1470 when his former ally the Earl of Warwick (the 'Kingmaker') switched sides to bring about a short-lived restoration of Henry VI.

But Edward IV regained the throne in 1471 after the Battle of Tewkesbury.

Henry's son Edward was killed in the battle and this quickly led to Henry's murder in the Tower of London in 1471.

Edward's personal position appeared to be secure, but he died suddenly of pneumonia in 1483. He nominated his brother Richard as Lord High Protector of the Realm to act as regent for his son Edward – he could not have foreseen that Richard would stage a coup and take the throne for himself.

EDWARD V

1470–1483, never crowned, 'reigned' 9 Apr–25 June 1483
Son of Edward IV and Elizabeth Woodville

Twelve-year-old Prince Edward was the rightful heir to the throne after his father Edward IV's sudden death in 1483. He was living at Ludlow Castle, and his mother, Queen Elizabeth Woodville, insisted that he should be given protection on his journey down to London.

Richard, Duke of Gloucester, had been named as Lord High Protector of the Realm in Edward IV's will, and Elizabeth wanted to arrange a coronation for her son as quickly as possible. But Richard was aware of this and hurried south to intercept the prince's party, and he ordered many of them to be arrested. In May, Richard and the uncrowned king arrived in London and Edward was taken to apartments in the Tower of London.

Elizabeth found sanctuary at Westminster Abbey with her other children, but the Duke of Gloucester then insisted that Richard, Edward's nine-year-old younger brother, should also be taken away and put in the Tower with his brother.

Richard started a campaign to prove that the two princes were illegitimate on the grounds that Edward IV's marriage to Elizabeth Woodville was bigamous because he was betrothed to someone else at the time of their marriage. However spurious the argument, Parliament accepted it and Richard became the legal heir to the throne.

Within three weeks, the duke had himself crowned Richard III. Edward V had been king for two months, although he was never crowned.

It is clear that anyone who wanted to be king would have to get both of these young princes out of the way. The finger of history clearly points at their uncle Richard. The princes in the Tower just disappeared. Two hundred years later, some human bones were discovered in the Tower, and Charles II ordered them to be interred in Westminster Abbey.

One nobleman, Lord Hastings, expressed misgivings about events at the time; he was arrested at a council meeting and Richard had him beheaded on the spot. That seemed to have the desired effect of dampening down any more criticism.

“

Farewell, my own sweet son.
God send you good keeping,
let me kiss you 'ere you go, for
God knoweth where we shall
kiss together again.

ELIZABETH WOODVILLE'S LAST WORDS
TO HER NINE-YEAR-OLD SON, PRINCE RICHARD,
AS HE WAS TAKEN AWAY TO THE TOWER.
SHE NEVER SAW HER SONS AGAIN.

RICHARD III

1452–1485, reigned 1483–1485
Son of Richard, Duke of York,
and Cecily Neville

If any English monarch has had a bad press (and quite a few have), it is Richard III, the former Duke of Gloucester, who must come top. Shakespeare describes him as a villainous hunchback and virtually all Tudor writers describe him as an ugly, evil monster.

Shakespeare was writing in the reign of Queen Elizabeth I, granddaughter of Henry VII-to-be, and it would have been unwise of him to portray Richard as anything but a murderous villain. He certainly managed that.

Richard III will be forever accused of murdering the two young princes Edward and Richard in the Tower. There is no evidence that they were indeed murdered; they just disappeared. But Richard did profit handsomely from their disappearance – although he was supposed to be the guardian of their welfare, he suddenly claimed the throne. And having become king, he did not achieve popularity: he executed his enemies without trial and confiscated their land.

⚜ MY KINGDOM FOR A HORSE!

A young Welshman, Henry Tudor, Earl of Richmond, claimed the throne was rightfully his in 1483, and both the Houses of Lancaster and York united behind him. Henry had been living in Brittany watching events unfold, and on 1 August 1485, he set out from France with a small army of French mercenaries.

He landed at Milford Haven, not far from Pembroke where he was born, and marched up through West and Mid-Wales and the Marches, gaining supporters all the way, to engage Richard at the Battle of Bosworth Field in Leicestershire on 22 August 1485.

Richard's only hope was Lord Stanley, one of the most powerful lords in England. He refused to commit to either side until it was clear who was going to win – and then duly entered the battle on the day on the side of Henry.

Richard was courageous in battle and came close to engaging Henry in combat before being cut down himself. Shakespeare has him pleading: 'A horse, a horse! My kingdom for a horse!' Legend has it that Lord Stanley picked up Richard's crown from a thorn bush on the battlefield and placed it on Henry's head.

Richard's body was slung over a horse and taken to Leicester for a crude burial at the Greyfriars Friary. In 2012, during a state-of-the-art archaeological dig, his remains were discovered under a long-stay car park in Leicester and, after much negotiation, were eventually reinterred in Leicester Cathedral in 2015.

66 ·

Now is the winter of our discontent
Made glorious summer by this sun of York;
And all the clouds that lour'd upon our house
In the deep bosom of the ocean buried.

THE OPENING LINES OF SHAKESPEARE'S
***RICHARD III,* SPOKEN BY RICHARD,**
DESCRIBING HIS BROTHER EDWARD AS THIS SON,
OR SUN, OF YORK

· ·

HOUSE OF TUDOR

HENRY VII

1457–1509, reigned 1485–1509
Son of Edmund Tudor and
Margaret Beaufort

Henry Tudor's paternal grandfather was Owen Tudor, an attendant to Henry V who fell in love with Henry's queen, Catherine of Valois, after Henry V died. They married in great secrecy and the couple had five children (rather remarkably) before their secret came out. Owen, one of the Tudors of Penmynydd, Anglesey, was described in a chronicle at the time as a 'goodly gentilman and beautyful person, garnished with many godly gifts, both of nature and of grace'.

Owen's son Edmund Tudor married Margaret Beaufort and she was only 13 when she gave birth to the future Henry VII. Sadly, she was already a widow at the time of Henry's birth – Edmund, who became the 1st Earl of Richmond, had died as a prisoner of the Yorkists in 1456.

Margaret was the great-great-granddaughter of Edward III, and was descended from John of Gaunt, Duke of Lancaster. Henry never knew his father but after Henry VI was killed in 1471, the future Henry VII became the head of the House of Lancaster and a figure of great importance because he was, as Edward IV put it, 'the only imp now left of Henry VI's brood'.

Henry Tudor was born at Pembroke Castle and brought up at Raglan Castle in Wales and for security reasons, after Henry VI was killed, was taken into exile for 14 years in Brittany by his uncle and guardian, Jasper, Earl of Pembroke. He was a king in waiting.

It was a masterstroke by Henry to marry Edward IV's daughter, Elizabeth of York. In 1483, two years before the Battle of Bosworth, Henry had pledged in Rennes Cathedral that when he became King of England he would marry Princess Elizabeth of York, heiress of the House of York, and he did so in 1486.

The union served to successfully unite the Houses of Lancaster and York. The new emblem was the Tudor Rose, made up of both red and white roses.

The marriage was a very happy one and the king and queen became a devoted couple. Henry was totally faithful, by all accounts – something of a rarity at the time.

Elizabeth gave birth to their first child at Winchester in 1488, a son who they christened Arthur, after the legendary king. Arthur later married a Spanish princess in 1501, but he died five months later, aged just 15, at Ludlow Castle. The cause of his death was probably tuberculosis. The younger son, the future Henry VIII, became the heir to the throne. Prince Henry then married Arthur's young widow, Catherine of Aragon. This union was to have fateful consequences. It is interesting to wonder what would have happened if Arthur had lived and Henry had never taken the throne. The history of England would almost certainly have been very different.

The marriage of Henry VII's eldest daughter, Margaret, to James IV of Scotland, would also have repercussions later, as the marriage connected the royal families of England and Scotland, leading the Stuarts to the throne when the Tudor dynasty came to an end.

In 1503, Henry VII's wife, Elizabeth, died in childbirth. The King was distraught, having lost his eldest child and his beloved wife in quick succession. He withdrew into matters of administration in his later years: he doubled the crown revenue and oversaw a peace that lasted for the 24 years of his reign.

One of Henry's legacies was the Lady Chapel (the Henry VII chapel) in Westminster Abbey. The Lady Chapel, begun in 1503 and consecrated in 1516, is the last great masterpiece of English medieval architecture. In 1545, historian John Leland called it 'the wonder of the entire world'. The outstanding feature of the chapel is the breathtaking fan-vaulted roof with its carved pendants. Around the walls are 95 statues of saints. Behind the altar is the tomb of Henry VII and his Queen Elizabeth. He died aged 52 and his teenage son Henry took the crown.

 ## YOU LOSE SOME, YOU LOSE SOME

Henry was assiduous in building up the country's finances and was assisted by John Morton, who was made Lord Chancellor in 1487. Nobody was to be exempted from taxes. A principle known as 'Morton's Fork' made sure of that:

> If the subject is seen to live frugally, tell him because he is clearly a money saver of great ability, he can afford to give generously to the King. If,

however, the subject lives a life of great extravagance, tell him he, too, can afford to give largely, the proof of his opulence being evident in his expenditure.

Heads you lose, tails you lose for the taxpayer. Heads you win, tails you win for the King.

Morton was 450 years ahead of Joseph Heller's masterpiece *Catch-22*.

 ## THE YEOMAN OF THE GUARD

Security was always in Henry's mind, and in 1485, he formed a personal bodyguard from his followers known as the 'Yeomen of the Guard', today the oldest British military corps in existence.

The Queen's Body Guard of the Yeomen of the Guard (to give it its full name) was created in 1485 at the Battle of Bosworth. Today they have a purely ceremonial role at royal garden parties and such, their most famous duty perhaps being to search the cellars of Westminster Palace before the State Opening of Parliament.

The Yeomen of the Guard are often confused with the Yeomen Warders of Her Majesty's Royal Palace and Fortress the Tower of London (to give it its full name) who are popularly known as Beefeaters, and who are based at the Tower of London.

HENRY VIII

1491–1547, reigned 1509–1547
Son of Henry VII and Elizabeth
of York

Henry VIII is England's most popular and famous king, being most famous for having six wives. This is still the record for an English king. He is almost a fictional figure, which is not surprising considering the number of fictional accounts in which he has been the central character.

Henry was a giant among kings. He was 17 when he came to the throne, well over six feet tall, slim (in the early days), athletic, charming, well-educated, speaking French and Latin, and some Spanish and Italian. As the second son, it was not expected that he would make it to the throne at all. Henry had been destined for a religious life, possibly to become Archbishop of Canterbury. When Prince Arthur died suddenly in 1502, Henry swiftly married his widow, an attractive Spanish princess, Catherine of Aragon. She was 23 at the time, and famed for her beauty. By marrying his sister-in-law, Henry had retained her healthy dowry. The House of Tudor desperately needed money, as well as needing a son and heir to cement the succession. This was to cause one or two problems later on.

⚜ HENRY'S QUEST FOR A SON

Catherine fell pregnant eight times, but had only one baby – a daughter Mary (later Mary I) – and as the years went on, the need for a son grew even more desperate.

Meanwhile, Henry fell in love with Anne Boleyn, who insisted on marrying him, refusing to become his mistress, so the King did everything he could to get a divorce. The only reason he could come up with was that Catherine had been his sister-in-law before their marriage and that it was against church law to marry one's brother's wife.

Henry asked Pope Clement VII to annul the marriage, but he refused to do so – on the grounds that Henry had already applied for special dispensation to bend church law to marry Catherine in the first place!

Henry VIII's chief minister was Thomas Wolsey, who went on to become Archbishop of York and harboured hopes at one time of becoming Pope. But Wolsey's failure to have the marriage annulled turned the King and Anne Boleyn against him. He was charged with treason, and died on his way to trial in 1530.

In 1533, Archbishop Thomas Cranmer of Canterbury did annul the marriage to Catherine, and Anne was crowned queen. Their daughter, Elizabeth (later Elizabeth I), was born three months later. The Pope excommunicated Henry, but it did not seem to overly bother him.

Anne Boleyn enjoyed a three-year marriage with Henry but her inability to bear a son would seal her fate. Charges were made of incest with her brother and of adultery with four other lovers. There were also whispers of witchcraft and she was beheaded in 1536. Her daughter, Elizabeth, was declared a bastard.

Henry had better luck with the next wife: Jane Seymour, lady-in-waiting to Anne Boleyn, who did produce a much-wanted son, Edward (later Edward VI), but she died 12 days after giving birth. Henry was heartbroken.

Thomas Cromwell, Henry's chief minister from 1532 to 1540, made an uncharacteristic mistake in 1539. For political reasons, he suggested an 'attractive' German princess, Anne of Cleves, as Henry's next wife. Holbein had painted a flattering portrait of her, but Henry found her dull and ugly when he met her, describing her as the 'Mare of Flanders'. He did marry her, but he refused to consummate the marriage, which was annulled seven months later in 1540.

Henry fell in love again and 18-year-old Catherine Howard, a lively girl, became his fifth wife. They were married on 28 July 1540, the same day that Cromwell was beheaded as a traitor and a heretic. Unfortunately, his second Catherine was a bit too lively for Henry, who had her beheaded for adultery.

Lesser men may have given up on the institution of marriage by now (he had an heir after all) but he chanced upon Catherine Parr, twice widowed and still only 31.

 KEEPING UP WITH THE TUDORS

This famous mnemonic describes the fates of Henry's six wives:

Divorced

Beheaded

Died

Divorced

Beheaded

Survived

This looks like a neat mnemonic; unfortunately, it's wrong! Henry's first and fourth marriages did not end in divorce, they were annulled. (A divorce ends a legally valid marriage, an annulment treats the marriage as if it never existed.) And this is a way to remember their first names:

Kate and Anne and Jane

And Anne and Kate (again, again)

⚜ THE DISSOLUTION OF THE MONASTERIES

Henry's marriages are what most people remember about him and it was the marriages and annulments that were the catalyst for huge changes in the religious and social life of the country.

Henry had declared himself head of the Church in England in 1530, breaking with the Pope over his annulment with Catherine of Aragon. Henry was declared Supreme Head of the Church of England in the Act of Supremacy 1534. Sir Thomas More refused to recognise him as the Supreme Head and was convicted of treason and executed. Henry was now in the very convenient and very comfortable position of being able to annul his own marriage (or marriages).

In 1536, Henry personally introduced a bill in Parliament in 1536 to destroy the monasteries. This was to result in the biggest redistribution of land since the Normans. Henry's Master Secretary Cromwell relentlessly pushed through the Dissolution of the Monasteries.

In 1537, the smaller monasteries were closed and by 1539, all 823 abbeys and monasteries – home to 9,000 monks and nuns – throughout the kingdom were dissolved in what was one of the biggest and most far-reaching changes in British history. The estates, estimated to make up one quarter of the country's land, including the massive wealth that they held and represented, went to the Crown.

The king's men looted the monasteries, appropriating anything worth stealing and hundreds of beautiful buildings were destroyed. In one fell swoop, Henry had destroyed the power of Catholicism in England and in the process, acquired massive riches for the Crown.

He used this income to make improvements to many royal buildings, especially Hampton Court Palace. He developed his father's chapel at Westminster Abbey, the Henry VII chapel, founded Trinity College, Cambridge and oversaw the interior of King's College

Chapel, Cambridge, with its Tudor emblems and the initials of H and A (Henry and Anne) carved on a wooden screen leading to the choir.

 WHAT'S IN A NAME?

Fidei defensor, Defender of the Faith, has been a subsidiary title of the English monarchy since 1521 when it was granted by Pope Leo X to Henry VIII. After Henry's decision to break with Rome in 1530, the title was revoked.

However, in 1544, Parliament conferred the title of Defender of the Faith on Henry VIII and his successors. The abbreviation *Fid Def* has appeared on British coins since 1715, today sometimes abbreviated as *F. D.*

 MARY ROSE (AND SANK AND ROSE AGAIN)

Henry greatly developed the navy, increasing its size from five ships to 53, and built some majestic warships including *Harry Grace a Dieu*, which had five decks and 200 cannons, and his flagship the *Mary Rose*, which sank at the Battle of the Solent. It was salvaged in 1982. In the 1520s Henry established the Navy Royal, forerunner of the Royal Navy, and set up a naval dock at Portsmouth.

EDWARD VI

1537–1553, reigned 1547–1553
Son of Henry VIII and
Jane Seymour

Edward was only nine when he took the throne, and 15 when he died. Both his parents were dead, and two stepmothers were lost (one annulled and one beheaded) before he was four.

His mother's brother Edward Seymour, Duke of Somerset, took the title of Lord Protector. In 1549, when Edward was king, Somerset lost out in a power struggle and John Dudley, Earl of Warwick, who created himself Duke of Northumberland, took on the role of Protector. Edward, 15 years old at the time, noted in an icily matter-of-fact entry in his diary in 1552: 'Somerset had his head cut off.'

Edward took a great interest in religious matters and was a fierce supporter of Protestantism, taking great pleasure in discussing the issues with the bishops of the day.

Under Edward's direction, Parliament passed the Act of Uniformity in 1549. Many Catholic rituals were banned and Holy Communion (Mass, matins and evensong) had to be conducted in English. This formalised reforms that had been brought in from 1547. All icons of stone or wood, carved or painted, were to be removed and wall-paintings to be whitewashed over.

The First Book of Common Prayer was introduced in 1549 containing in English the wording of prayers and the order of service to be used throughout the kingdom in place of the old Catholic practices. It was largely the work of the Archbishop of Canterbury, Thomas Cranmer, and was a mixture of Catholic and Lutheran beliefs. It was extensively revised in 1552 and much of its tradition and language remains in the Church of England today.

People used to pay money to have Masses said for them after their death. Protestants no longer believed in saying prayers for the dead, and the Dissolution of the Chantries Act put an end to this custom in the Anglican church.

Chantries had played a key part in helping to provide education, which was seriously affected as a result of the act. Edward was personally involved in establishing grammar schools to make up the loss. To this day, there are a good number of King Edward VI schools dating from this time.

In 1552, Edward suffered a bout of smallpox and then contracted tuberculosis. He died the following year. Edward VI's last words were reported to be: 'O my Lord God, defend this realm from Papistry.' He would have been extremely angry had he known that his half-sister, Mary I, a Catholic, would succeed him.

DID YOU KNOW?

In common with other princes at the time, Edward had a whipping boy. This was an unenviable role that involved being whipped by a tutor or governor for some misdemeanour/mistake that the king/prince had made. The tutor would not dare to punish the king/prince, the Lord's anointed, and so the proxy took one for the prince. Edward's whipping boy was Barnaby Fitzpatrick and they became good friends. This whipping boy became the 2nd Baron of Upper Ossory.

⚜ LADY JANE GRAY

Lady Jane Gray is perhaps the saddest and most tragic figure in the whole history of the English monarchy. She was the Nine-Day Queen, who was pitilessly and cruelly manipulated into being declared queen on the death of her second cousin, Edward VI.

She was born in 1537 to the Duke and Duchess of Suffolk and executed in 1554.

A great-granddaughter of Henry VII, Lady Jane had lived with royalty all her life.

She was attractive and intelligent, exactly the same age as Edward VI and one of a small number of his young friends. Catherine Parr helped in her education, and the future queens, Mary and Elizabeth, cousins of her mother, treated her kindly. Elizabeth was only five years older than Jane, and regarded her as a younger sister.

She preferred reading Plato in Greek to hunting on her father's estate at Bradgate Park, Leicester. In fact, had Edward VI lived, she might well have married him.

Henry VIII had made the line of succession clear: after his death, Edward was to become king, and if necessary (i.e. if Edward died without an heir), the throne would pass successively to his daughters Mary and Elizabeth.

Edward VI's Lord Protector, the Duke of Northumberland, is the villain of the piece. When he discovered the King was dying, he persuaded him to 'devise the throne' to Lady Jane because she was a staunch Protestant. At the same time, he persuaded Jane's parents to marry their daughter to his son, Lord Guilford Dudley. His scheming had the dual purpose of preventing the Catholic Mary taking the throne, and also neatly bolstering his power by being the father of the king consort.

Jane was shamefully bullied into it and was furious when told she was to become queen: 'The crown is not my right. And pleaseth me not. The Lady Mary is the rightful heir.' She was queen from 10 July until 19 July 1553.

Mary was in Norfolk and organised an army to march on London and nine days after Lady Jane has been proclaimed queen, she herself claimed the throne with great popular support. Most of the royal council proclaimed Mary as queen. Northumberland was executed immediately.

Jane was delighted with the news that she was not to be queen and it is reported that the she said something along the lines of 'Can I go home now?' Unfortunately, but not surprisingly, the answer was 'No'. Jane was kept prisoner in the Tower for six months.

One day, from her room, she saw the decapitated body of her teenage husband being taken away in a handcart. She knew that within minutes, it was her turn to suffer the same fate and be wheeled away into history.

Jane died, it is said, very bravely. On the scaffold, she pleaded with the executioner, 'Please despatch me quickly.' She tied her kerchief round her eyes and felt for the block saying, 'Where is it?' One of the onlookers guided her to the block where she laid her head down, and stretched out her arms saying, 'Lord, into thy hands I commend my spirit' – according to the Gospel of St Luke, the last words of Jesus.

MARY I

1516–1558, reigned 1553–1558
Daughter of Henry VIII and
Catherine of Aragon

Mary endured a very unhappy childhood. Her mother, Catherine, was banished from court; she was declared a bastard by her father; she saw her father marry Anne Boleyn, and then behead her. Her second stepmother died after childbirth, her third stepmother was ill-treated by her father and then a fourth stepmother was beheaded.

After her father's death, Mary found her fiercely Protestant little half-brother Edward, her new king, both precocious and insufferable.

Mary was 37 when she was crowned. She was the first Queen Regnant (that is a queen reigning in her own right rather than through marriage) and she was determined to restore the Catholic faith to England.

In her late thirties, she thought her best bet for marriage would be Philip of Spain, son and heir of the Catholic Charles V, to whom she had once been betrothed herself. They were married in an extravagant and lavish ceremony in Winchester Cathedral in 1554. Two years later, he became King Philip II of Spain, which made Mary Queen of Spain.

But that was the high point. Philip could not conceal his disdain for her, a 38-year-old virgin, and flirted with her ladies-in-waiting, as well as with her half-sister Elizabeth. He left England as soon as he could after the wedding and returned just once for a few weeks.

The marriage provoked much anti-Spanish and anti-Catholic sentiment and caused a rebellion among the Protestants in Kent. Two Protestant bishops were burned at the stake in Oxford in 1555, followed by Archbishop Cranmer of Canterbury the following year.

Mary restored papal supremacy and the heresy laws were reintroduced. Heresy was regarded as a religious and civil offence amounting to treason. She was determined to rid England of Protestants, and many cruelties were committed in her name; across the country, around 300 Protestant heretics who refused to give up their religion were burnt at the stake in three years.

Foxe's *Book of Martyrs* published in 1563 gives a detailed record of burnings at the stake:

> There were burnt 5 bishops, 21 divines, 8 gentlemen, 84 artificers, 100 husbandmen, servants and labourers, 26 wives, 9 virgins, 2 boys and 2 infants. 64 more were persecuted for their religion, whereof 7 were whipped, 16 perished in prison and 12 were buried in dunghills.

Not for nothing was she known as Bloody Mary. The most fundamental effect of this policy, and for the queen herself, was an intense and long-lasting fear and loathing of Catholics and Catholicism.

There was great rejoicing when she died in 1558 aged 42 and people celebrated the prospect of her half-sister Elizabeth taking the throne.

LOSING FRANCE FOREVER

In 1558, the last year of Mary's reign, England lost Calais – the last relic of empire that the English had held since 1347. It was a great military blunder. When the news reached the Queen, she is reported to have said, 'When I am dead and opened, you shall find Philip and Calais lying in my heart.'

Calais had been seen up to that point as a permanent part of England. An inscription over one of the town gates read:

> Then shalle the Frenchmen Calais winne,
> When iron and leade lyke corke shall swimme

In 1407, one Richard Whittington, the famous Lord Mayor of London known from the famous folk tale, had been Mayor of Calais as well as London.

ELIZABETH I

1533–1603, reigned 1558–1603
Daughter of Henry VIII
and Ann Boleyn

Queen Elizabeth was one of the great monarchs of England. She has fascinated historians for centuries, and more books have been written about her than any other English king or queen –

and more films made too. She was 25 when she was crowned, and was to rule for 45 years.

She had had a similarly disturbing upbringing to her elder sister, Mary: she was only two when her mother Anne Boleyn was beheaded; she saw four stepmothers die – the first in childbirth, the second annulled, the next beheaded and finally, Catherine Parr, who died in childbirth after she remarried following the death of Henry VIII.

Elizabeth grew up in uncertain times. Her worst moment was during Mary I's reign when she was taken prisoner at the Tower under suspicion of treason in 1553.

She refused to enter the Tower by Traitors' Gate. 'I come in as no traitor, but as true a woman to the Queen's majesty as any now living.' Nonetheless, she was imprisoned in the Tower for two months and narrowly escaped being executed.

Mary later sent her to Woodstock Palace along with 60 soldiers to guard her. It was a miserable time. She plaintively scratched a message with a diamond on a window at Woodstock in 1555:

> Much suspected by me,
> Nothing proved can be,
> Quoth Elizabeth, prisoner.

Elizabeth was a consummate practitioner of royalty. She had a first-class mind coupled with good judgment – qualities that all too rarely go together. She learned the best ways to survive; and most importantly, that it was prudent to be diplomatic. She learned in short how to be queen.

And she knew the power of PR and public image. Elizabeth forked out £16,000 of her own money to pay for her coronation in 1559. She dressed the part spectacularly throughout her reign, owning more than 250 gowns, all expensively bejewelled, judging from the many paintings of her. It took two hours for her to get ready to be seen at court.

One of her principles of royalty was to make regular tours, called progresses, around the country, staying with loyal subjects, and often arriving on horseback rather than by carriage. This practice kept Elizabeth in the public eye, and the locals always loved her visits and the entertainment that went with them. Once she stayed at Kenilworth Castle for three weeks as the guest of her good friend Robert Dudley, Earl of Leicester. Preparations for the visit took some years – new apartments were built for the Queen and her huge entourage. A visit from the Queen was clearly a privilege and also, just as clearly, very expensive – the host had to foot the bill. The Earl of Leicester was practically bankrupted, but it was deemed to be money well spent.

⚜ MARY, QUEEN OF SCOTS

Mary Stuart was born in 1542, the daughter of James V of Scotland, and Mary, daughter of the Duke of Guise. Her father died in battle fighting the English and she was one week old on her accession to the Scottish throne. She married Francis, Dauphin of France, in 1558, and the following year, the Catholic Mary became Queen of France when her husband became King Francis II of France.

When Francis died in 1560, Mary returned to a fiercely Protestant Scotland and married Lord Darnley, a Scottish nobleman. There was a murder plot in which she may or may not have been implicated, but in 1567 she was forced to leave Scotland and flee to England. She was captured in 1568 and imprisoned at Carlisle Castle by Elizabeth.

Elizabeth's ministers urged her to execute Mary, but the Queen was loath to kill another queen – and one who was her cousin. It was the one issue in her life on which she wavered. Mary was imprisoned for 19 years, and the two never met, although they wrote gentle letters to each other.

In 1586, the Babington Plot was uncovered – a Catholic conspiracy to murder Queen Elizabeth and for a Spanish army to invade England. Mary was corresponding with the plotters and this was too much for Elizabeth: Mary was tried, found guilty of treason and executed at Fotheringhay Castle in 1587.

66 . . . .

Just look how well she governs;
she is only a woman, only mistress
of half an island, and yet she makes
herself feared by Spain, by France,
by the Empire, by all.

**POPE SIXTUS V, ON
ELIZABETH I IN 1585.**

. . . .

All through her reign Elizabeth used her sexuality and virginity as instruments of power and intrigue. Who would she marry? There were plenty of would-be suitors: Philip of Spain, the Archduke of Austria, Robert Dudley, Earl of Leicester... but the years slipped away. The Virgin Queen she remained, almost becoming a Protestant substitute for the Virgin Mary. And she was happy with that: 'I would rather be a beggar and single, than a queen and married,' she wrote in 1563.

Elizabeth's reign was a golden age. Elizabeth cannot be given personal credit for the works of Shakespeare, Johnson, Spenser, Donne, Marlow, Tallis, Byrd, or the exploits of her adventurers like Drake and Raleigh, but she presided over a court and a country in which these activities and achievements were appreciated, and encouraged to flourish and prosper.

⚜ THE SPANISH ARMADA

Francis Drake became the first Englishman to sail around the world – it took him three years from 1577 to 1580. The Spanish called him El Draque – the Dragon.

He sailed with five ships, but by the time he reached the Pacific Ocean in October 1578 only one was left, his flagship the *Pelican*, renamed the *Golden Hind*.

In 1588, after Mary Queen of Scots' execution the year before, Philip II of Spain mounted a vast fleet – an armada – to sail to the Netherlands from Cadiz and then to invade England, overthrow Elizabeth and re-establish Catholicism. A fleet of 130 Spanish ships set sail with 8,000 sailors and 18,000 soldiers and was met by the English fleet led by Lord Howard with Drake as his vice admiral. It was the largest assault on England for 700 years. The English harried the Spanish as they sailed up the Channel until they reached Calais, where the Spanish fleet was scattered by an English attack of eight fireships.

The two fleets met at the Battle of Gravelines off Flanders, with the English destroying a number of Spanish ships. Strong winds prevented the Spanish picking up the rest of their army in the Netherlands, and they ended up being blown around the British Isles in severe gale force winds. Many Spanish ships were wrecked on the way home off the west coast of Ireland.

Queen Elizabeth met her troops, who were stationed at Tilbury Camp to defend the country from what was an invasion on an unprecedented scale. She rose to the occasion:

> I know I have the body but of a weak and feeble woman;
> but I have the heart and stomach of a king, and of a king
> of England too, and think foul scorn that Parma or Spain,
> or any prince of Europe, should dare to invade the borders
> of my realm.

The speech has rightly been adjudged one of the greatest ever made by an English monarch. Who needs Shakespeare?

England's victory over the Spanish was seen as divine deliverance – one of the country's greatest military victories – and the boost to English national pride lasted for years. Sir Walter Raleigh named a prime piece of American real estate after her – Virginia. The Queen was pleased, even amused, perhaps.

Elizabeth's last speech to Parliament in 1601 serves as a fitting epitaph for the Virgin Queen. She was 68 and in failing health, and had reigned for 43 years. She was an expert of rhetoric and the speech was immediately called Queen Elizabeth's golden speech:

> [...] for it is not my desire to liue or reign longer, than my life & reigne shall bee for your good. And though you haue had, and may haue, many mightier and wiser Princes sitting in this Seat, yet you neuer had, nor shall haue, any that will loue you better.

She asked that all the 140 members of the Commons kiss her hand on the way out, and many of them were in tears. She died in 1603, and was buried in Westminster Abbey. On James I's orders, in 1606, her coffin was moved to a tomb in the north aisle of Henry VII's chapel and laid on top of the coffin of her half-sister, Mary. The inscription on the base of the monument says: 'Partners in throne and grave, here we sleep Elizabeth and Mary, sisters in hope of the Resurrection.'

HOUSE OF STUART

JAMES I

1566–1625, reigned 1603–1625
Son of Henry Stuart and
Mary, Queen of Scots
(James I of England also reigned as
James VI of Scotland from 1567–1625)

Elizabeth I had died without issue and this signified the end of the Tudor dynasty. Her successor was James VI of Scotland, who had already been on the Scottish throne for 36 years. He became James I of England, the first Stuart king.

For the first time, England, Scotland, Wales and Ireland were ruled by the same monarch.

James's claim to the throne came through his great-grandmother, Margaret Tudor, the daughter of Henry VII. He was crowned King of Scotland when he was 13 months old after his mother, Mary, Queen of Scots, was taken away and imprisoned in England. He never saw her again.

In 1603, James ascended the English throne, peacefully. He left Edinburgh for London and the English lords entertained him with lavish hospitality along the route south. James was amazed by the wealth of his new kingdom, announcing that he was 'swapping a stony couch for a deep feather bed'. He liked it so much that during his 22 years in England, he returned to Scotland only once.

Sir Walter Scott said of James that he was 'exceedingly like an old gander, running about and cackling all manner of nonsense'. Henry IV of France is said to have called him 'the wisest fool in Christendom'. Both quotations are apt, for James was learned yet ridiculous and clumsy, clownish and well-read, awkward and witty, feeble and blustering. He slobbered, had a speech impediment and a most unregal bearing: 'A lifetime of gluttony and immoderate drinking had much reshaped his head and body,' according to American historian David Price. He was married and had seven children, but was openly homosexual.

James I was a foremost exponent and defender of the Divine Right of Kings. This doctrine asserts that monarchs derive their right to rule directly from the will of God. Therefore, the monarch could not be held accountable for his or her actions by any earthly authority such as a parliament. Understandably, this did not go down too well with many members of Parliament. He ruled for long periods without Parliament.

His lack of popularity extended beyond the governing classes: James aimed to convert everybody to Protestantism, and it was not long before unrest set in with a number of Catholics plotting against the King.

⚜ GUNPOWDER, TREASON AND PLOT

The most audacious and famous plan was what became known as the Gunpowder Plot: a conspiracy to blow up the Houses of

Parliament and King James at the State Opening of Parliament in 1605. One of the conspirators tipped off a fellow Catholic, who immediately told the authorities. Around midnight on 5 November 1605, soldiers searched the cellars of Parliament and caught Guy Fawkes red-handed, with 36 barrels of gunpowder – and a smoking gun, or rather a length of slow taper in his hand. The 12 plotters were rounded up, tortured and executed. An American newspaper at the time would have reported the terrorist incident as 11/5.

King James ordered that the event should be commemorated and celebrated every year and he commissioned an annual Gunpowder Plot sermon by a leading churchman. The date has gone down in British history, and remains the subject of a common nursery rhyme:

> Remember, remember!
> The fifth of November,
> The Gunpowder Treason and Plot.
> I know of no reason
> Why the Gunpowder Treason
> Should ever be forgot!

Bonfire Night became a national holiday for more than 200 years, celebrated by fireworks and the burning of effigies of Guy Fawkes, and sometimes the Pope.

James I was the first monarch to call himself King of Great Britain. A new flag representing this royal union between England and Scotland was introduced in April 1606 – it joined together the red Cross of St George of England on a white background with the white Cross of St Andrew of Scotland on a blue background. It was known simply as 'the British flag' or 'the flag of Britain'.

The Welsh dragon does not appear on the Union Flag because when the flag was created, Wales was already united with England and no longer a separate principality.

James I personally supervised the team of scholars who produced the authorised version of the Bible in 1611, one of the greatest and everlasting glories of the English language. A team of more than 50 scholars produced the translation that was reviewed by the bishops and then ratified by the King. The dedication to James was as 'principal mover and author of the work'. This edition of the Bible now takes his name in the title, the King James Authorised Version. It remains the most widely published text in the English language. And perhaps the most beautifully written.

James suffered from gout and arthritis, and died in 1625 aged 58 from a stroke.

 ## TO BOLDLY GO WHERE NO KING HAS GONE BEFORE

In 1620, James I scored a real first – he was the first English monarch to travel underwater in a... submarine! Come to think of it, he must have been the first monarch in the history of the planet to travel in a submarine.

Cornelius van Drebbel, a Dutch inventor who was working at the time for the Royal Navy under James I's patronage, had built a navigable submarine, and between 1620 and 1624 successfully built and tested two more.

The inventor took the King on a test dive beneath the Thames. The submarine could stay submerged for three hours and travel from Westminster to Greenwich and back, cruising at a depth of between 12 to 15 feet (4 to 5 metres).

CHARLES I

1600–1649, reigned 1625–1649
Son of James I and Anne of Denmark

Charles I is best remembered for being the only ruling English monarch put on trial by his opponents and then executed. On 30 January every year to commemorate his death, wreaths are placed round his statue in Trafalgar Square that looks down Whitehall to the place where he was executed.

He was the younger son of James I – the eldest son, Henry, Prince of Wales, died of typhoid after swimming in the Thames in 1612 and Charles, aged 12, became the heir. History would have taken a different road had Henry acceded to the throne – he seemed to have all the ability to be a fair and popular monarch. One thousand people marched behind his cortege to Westminster Abbey. His father, James I, did not attend – he did not like funerals.

Charles I's reign was not a happy one. His unbending and unyielding belief in the Divine Right of Kings coloured everything that happened during his reign, including his death. He was 'God's Lieutenant upon Earth' – as king, he viewed himself to be above the law.

Charles and his elegant French wife, Henrietta Maria, had two children, Charles and James, both future kings. They created a court that was sophisticated but autocratic. Charles constantly argued and disagreed with Parliament, generally over taxes; he dissolved Parliament three times, and for 11 years from 1629 to 1640, he attempted to run the country completely on his own.

In 1640, Charles was forced to recall Parliament – he needed money for a military campaign in Scotland. In the 'Grand

Remonstrance', a list of 204 complaints about the way he was ruling the country, Parliament publically rebuked Charles for his poor performance as king. Charles went to Westminster to personally arrest the five leaders of the Parliament only to find they had fled. 'All my birds have flown,' he said. They actually escaped in a boat on the Thames.

With tensions running so high across the kingdom, it was inevitable that civil war would break out – and it did in 1642. There followed seven years of battles, sieges and imprisonments, and Oliver Cromwell, MP for Huntingdon, found himself leading the Parliamentarians. It was estimated that one in five adult males took part in the fighting.

There were three major battles. Edge Hill in Warwickshire was an indecisive battle in 1642 but Charles lost control of the north of England when he lost the Battle of Marston Moor near York in 1644, where 3,000 Royalists were killed.

In June 1645, Cromwell, who had now become the leader of the Parliamentary forces, inflicted a decisive victory over Charles with his New Model Army at Naseby, Northamptonshire.

Charles never recovered. In 1646, the King tried to do a deal with the Scots, but they tricked him and sold him to Parliament for £400,000. The King escaped to Carisbrook Castle on the Isle of Wight and in 1648 a second civil war broke out. But it was short-lived after the Royalists were defeated at Preston in 1648.

Having being imprisoned for months, Charles was eventually tried in Westminster Hall before 50 members of Parliament 'for high crimes against the realm of England'. He maintained to the end that no court in England should try a king. 'The king can do no wrong.'

The sentence was announced: 'This Court doth adjudge that he the said Charles Stuart, as a Tyrant, Traitor, Murderer and Public Enemy to the good people of this Nation, shall be put to death, by the severing of his head from his body.'

On 30 January 1649, Charles I walked with his captors from St James's Palace to the Palace of Whitehall. It was a frosty morning, and he wore two shirts to keep him from shivering – he did not want to appear to be trembling or shaking with fear.

A wooden scaffold had been erected outside the Banqueting House in Whitehall, which he had built a few years earlier, and Charles spoke clearly and courageously to the crowds.

'I go from a corruptible to an incorruptible Crown, where no disturbances can be,' he said. There was a loud groan from the large crowd when the axeman brought down his blade. His body was interred at the Chapel of St George at Windsor.

⚜ OLIVER CROMWELL

Oliver Cromwell, MP for Huntingdon from 1628, became the Lord Protector of England in the Interregnum from 1649 to 1660. He was born in Huntingdon in 1599.

His grandfather Richard Williams was related to Thomas Cromwell, Henry VIII's chief minister, especially well known to readers of Hilary Mantel's *Wolf Hall*, and respected him so much that he changed his name from Williams to Cromwell in honour of Thomas.

When the Civil War began in 1642, Oliver Cromwell was an MP and a lowly cavalry captain but was quickly promoted and made lieutenant-general and commander of the cavalry of the parliamentary army. His cavalry charge won the day at Marston Moor.

In 1645, Parliament created the New Model Army, a 22,000-strong, national professional army to oppose the Royalists. The New Model Army was a different sort of fighting force – soldiers sang hymns before battle, listened to sermons and did not drink. The soldiers' discipline and sobriety and their religious belief made the army a very effective military unit: it had its greatest victory at Naseby taking 5,000 prisoners and £100,000 in jewels.

In the Civil War, Parliamentarians were referred to as Roundheads because many Puritan men had their hair cropped in a 'pudding basin cut'. Royalists were Cavaliers in reference to the Latin *caballarius* (horseman), and in *Henry IV, Part 2*, Shakespeare used the word to describe a haughty member of the gentry.

After Charles was executed in 1649, England was declared the Commonwealth and Free State of England ruled by a Council of State; the House of Lords and the monarchy were abolished. Cromwell became Chairman of the Council of State, and then in 1653, was proclaimed Lord Protector making him in effect a dictator. There was to be no monarch in England from 1649 to 1660 but Cromwell would be king in all but name from 1653. He was offered the title of king. He turned it down but nonetheless was addressed as Your Highness.

He imposed a strict and extreme puritanical religious regime upon the nation. Adultery was punished by death; no theatrical performances or games were allowed; taverns and brothels were closed down; and swearing and church ritual were both banned. All Sunday sports and non-religious activities were banned, including horseracing, cockfighting, bowling, shooting, dancing and wrestling. Dancing round the maypole was banned on any day.

Puritanical parliamentary soldiers wrecked many cathedrals and churches but the worst atrocities occurred in Ireland, with massacres at Wexford and a particularly brutal one at Drogheda in 1649, which have not been forgotten or forgiven in Ireland ever since.

Samuel Cooper painted a famous portrait in the 1650s of Cromwell, the most powerful living Englishman at the time. Cromwell was a realist, and at times he was humble too. He told the painter: 'The mirror does not flatter me. Nor should you, Mr Cooper. I'll have it warts and all.'

Cromwell's installation as Lord Protector was akin to a coronation, which saw him travelling in the Royal State Coach and sitting on a throne at Westminster Hall. He lived at Hampton Court like a monarch – the French ambassador was surprised to find Cromwell seated on a raised golden chair, wearing purple velvet edged with ermine.

On the night of 3 September 1658, during one of the most terrible storms London had ever seen, Cromwell died, aged 59. Diarist John Evelyn, clearly not a Cromwell fan, wrote of the funeral service at Westminster Abbey: 'The joyfullest funeral ever I saw. There was none that cried but dogs.'

Cromwell was, and remains to this day, a controversial figure that splits opinion. He was at once tolerant and intolerant, but he was a key figure in troubled times. Less than a year after his death, following the restoration of the monarchy, Cromwell was posthumously executed, his body dug up and chopped into pieces.

After his death, Cromwell's son Richard became Lord Protector II from September 1658 to May 1659. His father had nominated his son as his successor, which seems slightly out of character. Despite a grand installation ceremony, he struggled in the job and abdicated in 1659 and was forced to flee the country before Charles II returned to a joyous reception in 1660.

CHARLES II

1630–1685, reigned 1660–1685
(also King of Scotland, 1651–1685)
Son of Charles I and
Henrietta Maria of France

Charles arrived in London from the Netherlands in 1660 to claim the throne on his 30th birthday after years of exile during the Puritan Commonwealth. The majority of English people appeared to be very happy to have a king again and he received a joyous reception.

The Cromwell-hating John Evelyn reported in his diary of the arrival of Charles II back to London:

> He came with a triumph of over 20,000 horse and foot brandishing their swords and shouting with inexpressible joy. The ways were strewn with flowers, the bells were ringing, the streets were hung with tapestry, and the fountains were running with wine [...] the windows and balconies were all set with ladies, trumpets and music, and myriads of people flocked the streets as far as Rochester, so that they took seven hours to pass through the city. I stood in the Strand and beheld it and blessed God.

His welcome gives some idea of how much he was embraced, but the cheers for him were mixed with cheers, too, for the end of Puritanism. The people yearned for a change and they hoped Charles would deliver it. They had become weary of the dour puritanical life in the Interregnum. As Thomas Macauley wrote some time later: 'The Puritan hated bearbaiting not because it gave pain to the bear but because it gave pleasure to the spectators.'

Charles had spent a large part of his time before 1660 in exile or as a fugitive. He joined his mother in Paris after the Battle of Naseby in 1645 as the situation in England worsened. But after his father was executed, when he was 18, he theoretically succeeded to the throne. He attempted to regain the throne and was crowned King of Scotland in 1651, assembling an army of 17,000 troops to march south to England. Cromwell marched north and the two armies met at Worcester. Charles watched sadly from the tower of Worcester Cathedral as his army was defeated.

Fleeing from the battlefield, Charles was accompanied by a Royalist officer, Colonel William Carlos. On Carlos's advice, they both hid high up in an oak tree at Boscobel in Shropshire for 24 hours while Roundhead soldiers on the ground searched the woods for enemy soldiers. This is why so many pubs and inns all over England are called the Royal Oak, apparently now the third most common name in England for a pub. The tree is cared for today by English Heritage.

After that narrow escape, he fled south and later took shelter among the stones at Stonehenge, using a number of disguises, once as a manservant called William Jackson, before managing to cross the Channel to France and safety. He was to spend another nine years in exile.

⚜ THE MERRY MONARCH

Charles's exile in France had helped him develop some sophisticated tastes. Theatres, which had been closed during the Commonwealth, were reopened; and in 1662, he established the Royal Society, which promoted scientific ideas and research.

Charles was something of an amateur scientist himself and had a laboratory of sorts in Whitehall Palace. Later he helped to pay for the Royal Observatory at Greenwich (Christopher Wren advised him on its location) and also the Royal Hospital at Chelsea.

In 1666, the Great Fire of London started in a bakery in Pudding Lane and spread like wildfire through the wooden buildings. It destroyed 13,000 buildings including 87 churches and the fire lasted five days.

Charles II showed much courage and bravery in helping in the firefighting operations along with his brother, James, Duke of York. It was reported that at one time, King Charles, armed with a bucket and spade, ankles in water, helped to put out the flames.

The court went racing at Newmarket twice a year – Charles II played a part in making the town the premier horseracing centre in the country. He was a good horseman and his favourite stallion was called Old Rowley. That became one of the King's nicknames, and the Rowley Mile is the name of one of the racecourses at Newmarket to this day.

Charles married Catherine of Braganza in 1662. She brought a sizeable dowry: a large sum of money, Bombay and Tangier, and trading rights to the East Indies and China.

Charles and Catherine's three children were all stillborn, but Charles had a large number of mistresses and fathered nine sons and seven daughters out of wedlock. He treated them all well, giving them titles and honours. His sexual appetite was never hidden away from the people; rather it was lauded and appreciated. Charles was popular and brought a sense of fun to the monarchy that had long been missing. He was called the Merry Monarch and well deserved the epithet. At last, the fierce bigotry of the Puritans was over.

The most famous of Charles's mistresses was Nell Gwyn. She was brought up in a brothel in London and got a job selling oranges at theatres. She ended up on stage herself and became

Charles's mistress in 1668. The King set her up in a smart house in Pall Mall.

Charles Beauclerk was an illegitimate son of Charles by Nell. One story has it that on the arrival of the King one day, his mother said, 'Come here, you little bastard, and greet your father.' When the King rebuked her for calling him that, Nell replied, 'Your Majesty has given me no other name to call him by.' In response, Charles created him Earl of Burford on the spot, and then in 1684, the Duke of St Albans.

On another famous occasion, her coach was surrounded by a hostile crowd who mistook her for another of Charles's mistresses, the Roman Catholic Duchess of Portsmouth. Nell stuck her head out of the window and said: 'Pray good people, be silent. I am the Protestant whore.'

In 1681, he met the outlawed Quaker William Penn, the founder of Pennsylvania.

Penn refused to remove his hat when introduced to the King. Charles good- humouredly removed his own hat and said that it was the custom in these sort of meetings, 'for one of us to be bareheaded'.

 A KING'S BEST FRIEND

Charles was responsible for the popularity of a toy spaniel that took his name – the King Charles Spaniel. In his diary, Samuel Pepys describes how the dogs were allowed to roam freely around the palace at Whitehall, including during state occasions. In an entry dated 1 September 1666, describing a council meeting, Pepys wrote, 'All I observed there was the silliness of the King, playing with his dog all the while and not minding the business.'

JAMES II

1633–1701, reigned 1685–1688
Son of Charles I and Henrietta
Maria of France

James II has the dubious distinction of being the only King of England to be driven out of the land to die in exile, and also the last English monarch to be Catholic.

He reigned for four years and it is said that his incompetence led to the Glorious Revolution of 1688, which changed the nature of the monarchy forever.

Before James took the throne, he had proved to be an able and brave soldier, and accompanied his father on a number of missions. He oversaw a huge and successful expansion of the Royal Navy and as Duke of York directed the expedition that ended with England winning possession of Manhattan in 1664.

He converted to Catholicism in his thirties and a number of attempts were made to exclude him from the succession before Charles II died, but he ascended the throne in 1685. He immediately set out on a policy aimed at converting England to Roman Catholicism, in the process giving himself arbitrary and absolute powers. James refused to compromise with Parliament in any way.

Four months after he took the throne, the Duke of Monmouth, a Protestant, and an illegitimate son of Charles II, led a rebellion against James. The King's troops defeated the rebels in mass slaughter at the Battle of Sedgemoor in Somerset in 1685, the last battle to be fought between Englishmen on English soil. But it was to prove a pyrrhic victory.

Monmouth was executed along with 300 of his supporters. The trials became infamous and were known as the Bloody Assize – the harsh treatment meted out by Judge Jeffreys, known to history as 'the hanging judge', to the rebels made the King even more unpopular. Parliament responded by rejecting James's Declaration of Indulgence, which was aimed at abolishing the laws against Catholics.

James had two heirs by his first marriage to Anne Hyde: Princess Mary, and her younger sister, Anne. But out of the blue in 1688, and very conveniently for James, his second wife, Mary, gave birth to a son also named James. There was a Catholic heir to the throne at last. Or was there? Many people refused to believe that the baby was the King and Queen's, and one story spread about was that the infant had been smuggled into the Queen's bedroom at St James's Palace in a warming pan.

(After 'the warming-pan baby' incident, it was customary for the Home Secretary at the time to attend royal births to ensure the new baby was genuine and not an imposter. The last time a Home Secretary attended the birth of a future monarch was for the present Queen in 1926. The custom was halted before the birth of Prince Charles in 1948.)

⚜ THE GLORIOUS REVOLUTION

Immediately, a group of MPs, six lords and the Bishop of London – known as the Immortal Seven – invited Princess Mary's Dutch husband, the Protestant Prince William of Orange, to invade. 'Your Highness may be assured that there are 19 parts of 20 of the people throughout the kingdom who are desirous of a change,' they wrote.

It was an invitation to invasion and William of Orange could not refuse, leading the only successful invasion of England since the Norman Conquest. He landed at Brixham with 500 ships, including 53 warships and 15,000 men, in 1688, on what was an auspicious date for the Protestants – 5 November – and forced James to stand down. The invasion met with no opposition.

This was the Glorious Revolution, so named by the Whigs to celebrate the bloodlessness of the takeover and the assertion of the constitutional importance of Parliament. The monarchy was now a Parliamentary institution, and monarchs had to act in accordance with rules and conventions agreed by Parliament.

In December, Mary of Modena left London dressed as a washerwoman with 'the warming-pan baby' and fled to France. Eventually James followed her, and died in exile in France in 1701.

 TWENTY-SEVEN AND COUNTING

James II fathered 27 children, which appears to be the record for the royal family. He had eight with his first wife, Anne, 12 with his second wife Mary, including the warming-pan baby, four with one mistress and three with another. There were probably others. Samuel Pepys wrote that James was fond of his children and enjoyed his role as a father, which was unusual for the time. Pepys also wrote that he was reputed to be 'the most unguarded ogler of his time' and noted in his diary that on one occasion, the King even made a move on the diarist's wife: 'He did eye my wife mightily.'

HOUSE OF ORANGE AND STUART

WILLIAM III AND MARY II

William 1650–1702,
reigned 1689–1702
Son of William II, Prince of Orange,
and Mary, Princess of Orange

Mary 1662–1694, reigned 1689–1694
Daughter of James II and Anne Hyde

William and Mary were both grandchildren of Charles I and Henrietta Maria.

William was the son of Charles II's sister Mary, and Princess Mary was the daughter of James II by his first wife Anne Hyde.

Mary was only 15 when she was told she was to marry her cousin. She is said to have wept for days, and continued crying throughout the wedding ceremony in 1677. At six feet tall, she towered over her husband. Mary's sister Anne unkindly referred to him as Caliban, after Shakespeare's ogre in *The Tempest*.

At 'the putting the bride and bridegroom to bed ceremony', William refused to take off his underclothes as was the custom. After some argument with the father of the bride, Charles II drew the curtains round the bed and reportedly shouted, 'Now nephew to your work. Hey! St George for England!'

Parliament had appointed William and Mary to be joint sovereigns with William in overall charge. In 1689, the couple agreed to a Bill of Rights, which stated that all future monarchs had to be Protestant, and among other things, the monarch could not raise an army or raise taxes without the permission of Parliament. The balance of power had shifted significantly away from the monarchy.

Mary II was popular with the British people – she was after all British and a Protestant – but the same could not be said for William. His main interest was fighting a war against France and he spent most of the time on military missions in Europe.

With the support of Catholics in Ireland, Scotland and France, James II saw a chance to reclaim his crown, and he landed in northern Ireland in 1689 to try to seize control. He held Derry under siege, but was no match for William and his well-organised troops and on 1 July 1690, William III defeated James at the Battle of the Boyne, north of Dublin.

It was a crushing defeat for James, and secured the Protestant ascendancy in the north of Ireland for generations. The battle still retains huge symbolic importance in Northern Ireland, where it is celebrated by the Orange Order every 12 July.

In 1694, Mary died of smallpox and a lonely William, who said he never found a single fault in her, ruled on his own until he died in 1702. They had no children.

In February 1702, while out riding at Hampton Court, William's horse stumbled on a molehill and he was thrown, breaking his collarbone. His health, which had never been strong, deteriorated rapidly and he soon died. When courtiers undressed the King they found he was wearing Mary's wedding ring and a lock of her hair close to his heart.

Jacobite supporters of James II, who had died in exile the year before, did not mourn William and toasted the mole who made his horse fall as 'the little gentleman in the black velvet waistcoat'.

 ## LOCATION, LOCATION, LOCATION

William and Mary bought a property called Nottingham House in a little village outside London called Kensington, hoping that living in the country would be beneficial for their health. With the help of Sir Christopher Wren and Nicholas Hawksmoor, they transformed it into Kensington Palace.

ANNE

1665–1714, reigned 1702–1714
Daughter of James II and Anne Hyde

Queen Anne, Mary's sister, was married to Prince George of Denmark and spent much of her adult life in a state of being pregnant. She appears to have been pregnant every year from her wedding in 1683 until the time she ascended the throne in 1702.

She gave birth to 19 children, but only one survived childbirth, the Duke of Gloucester; he was to die of encephalitis when he was 11. The effect of the pregnancies on Anne's health must have been enormous. Life was hard and later she became seriously overweight.

It had become fairly obvious that Anne would die without an heir and Parliament feared that James II's son, also James, would attempt to take the throne. In 1701, Parliament passed the Act of Settlement, which established Hanoverian and Protestant succession to the throne. The act stipulated that if neither William III nor Queen Anne had direct heirs (as seemed very probable), the crown would pass to Anne's nearest Protestant relation, Princess Sophia, Electoress of Hanover, granddaughter of James I and first cousin to Charles II and James II.

The throne would then pass to her descendants, the principal purpose being to exclude Roman Catholics from the throne. The Act confirmed the Bill of Rights 1689: no Catholics or anybody married to a Catholic could sit on the throne.

However, Princess Sophia died in 1714, very shortly before Queen Anne, who did die childless. On Anne's death, Sophia's eldest son George, Elector of Hanover, succeeded to the throne as George I. His descendants, including our current queen, have ruled Britain ever since.

Parliament had passed the Act of Union in 1707, which extended the Act of Settlement to Scotland; England, Wales and Scotland were now united under one Parliament and the nation became the United Kingdom of Great Britain.

Towards the end of her life, Anne suffered from gout and could hardly walk. On her death in 1714, her body had become so large that she was buried in a coffin that was almost square.

YOUNG CHURCHILL

John Churchill, a young general, won a series of victories for the British against the French and Spanish in the War of the Spanish Succession. He became a national hero and the Queen bestowed on him the title of Duke of Marlborough and some land at Woodstock in Oxfordshire where he built a palace called Blenheim, named after one of his battles. Many generations of the Churchill family lived at Blenheim and Sir Winston Churchill was born there in 1874.

HOUSE OF HANOVER

GEORGE I

1660–1727, reigned 1714–1727
Son of Ernest Augustus and
Princess Sophia Dorothea of Celle

On the death of Queen Anne, Princess Sophia's eldest son became King George I of England at the age of 54.

In modern parlance, George I did not have much going for him. He seemed to hate most things, including England, the English, the English language, his wife and his children. And the English people didn't much like him either, and neither did anyone else.

When Princess Sophia Dorothea found out that she was to be married to George I, she shouted: 'I will not marry the pig snout!' George's mother, Sophia, was equally uncomplimentary, calling her son 'the most pigheaded, stubborn boy who ever lived, who has round his brains such a thick crust that I defy any man or woman ever to discover what is in them.'

In fact, the only thing that he did have going for him was that he was, at least, a Protestant.

For the entire duration of his reign, George I's wife, Sophia Dorothea, was imprisoned in Germany on suspicion of adultery. Their son, the future George II, was nine years old when his mother was incarcerated and he never forgave his father.

George I brought what were adjudged to be two of the ugliest mistresses ever to the English court: one short and fat, one tall and skinny. The short fat one was nicknamed the Elephant, and the tall skinny one the Maypole. Sometimes they were called Elephant and Castle.

One year after George I was crowned, a Jacobite Rebellion started in Scotland with the aim of putting the Old Pretender, James Francis Edward Stuart, heir to James II, on the throne. The Earl of Mar raised the Jacobite standard at Braemar in 1715 but the revolt soon fizzled out and the feeble rebellion was easily put down.

George I spent more time in Germany than England during his 12-year reign, and his German-ness had the unintended consequence of effecting a constitutional change of the first order. He could not be bothered dealing minutely with Parliament and so he entrusted his interests to a chief minister who he himself chose. Robert Walpole was appointed First Lord of the Treasury, a post he held until 1742 – Walpole was effectively the first Prime Minister.

After 1717, George rarely attended Cabinet meetings. This allowed the Cabinet to act collectively and formulate policies, which, provided they were backed by a majority in the Commons, the king was usually powerless to resist.

When George I died on a trip back to Germany in 1727, his death went uncommemorated in England.

PLAY IT AGAIN, GEORGE

George I had employed George Frederich Handel in Germany, and soon after the death of Queen Anne, the composer came to England to work for George I. George had a high regard for his fellow German. He employed him as a music teacher for his family, doubled his wages and in 1717, commissioned his *Water Music Suite*.

A newspaper at the time reported on the premiere:

At about 8 pm on Wednesday, 17 July, 1717, King George I and several aristocrats boarded a royal barge at Whitehall Palace for an excursion up the Thames toward Chelsea. The rising tide propelled the barge upstream without rowing. Another barge provided by the City of London contained about fifty musicians who performed Handel's music.

On arriving at Chelsea, the king left his barge, then returned to it at about 11 pm for the return trip. The king was so pleased with the Water Music that he ordered it to be repeated at least three times, both on the trip upstream to Chelsea and on the return.

GEORGE II

1683–1760, reigned 1727–1760
Son of George I and Sophia
Dorothea of Celle

George II had a very unhappy childhood – his mother was imprisoned by his father for alleged adultery when he was nine and her son never saw her again. She died in prison in 1726. George was at loggerheads with this father all his life and set up a rival court at St James's Palace with his wife, Caroline of Ansbach, when they were Prince and Princess of Wales.

George II was crowned at Westminster Abbey on 22 October 1727. Handel was commissioned to write four new anthems for the coronation, including the rousing Zadok the Priest coronation anthem no. 1, which has been played at every British coronation ever since. The words, from the Old Testament, have been used in every coronation service since Edmund the Elder's in 973. The anthem is the theme music for ITV's coverage of the European Champions League.

 GOD SAVE THE MUSIC-LOVING KING

George II is connected with another famous musical work, Handel's oratorio Messiah. No one really knows why or when the custom of standing during the

Hallelujah Chorus began. One theory is that George II, attending the London premiere in March 1743, was so moved by it that he stood up. Protocol is: if the king stands, everybody stands. There is no contemporaneous report that George did attend the premiere, but it would not have been surprising if he had, given that Handel was friendly with the King and on the royal payroll in the form of a pension.

The British national anthem has its origins during King George II's reign. The earliest version, 'God Save Great George Our King', was first heard in 1745 when the King attended a gala performance at Drury Lane Theatre in London in celebration of the defeat of Bonnie Prince Charlie.

⚜ GEORGE THE RECORD-BREAKER

George II holds three record lasts for the monarch: he was the last English monarch to be born abroad, he was the last English monarch to lead his troops on the battlefield, and he was the last monarch to be buried in Westminster Abbey.

He was distraught when his wife, Queen Caroline, died aged 54 in 1737 – he had slept on the floor of her bedroom when she was ill. It was said that after she died, he could not stand the sight of a queen in a pack of cards and that his daughter removed the queens from the pack before he played. When he died, George left instructions that the side-boards of each of their coffins be removed so the two could be joined together in death.

DID YOU KNOW?

The American state of Georgia was established in 1732, the last of the original Thirteen Colonies, and is named after George II.

In 1743, George II became the last British monarch to lead an army into battle, advancing on foot at the head of his infantry. At the age of 61, he led a joint force of British, German, Dutch and Austrian troops to victory over the French at the Battle of Dettingen in Bavaria during the War of the Austrian Succession.

'Don't tell me of danger,' he shouted to his troops. 'Now boys, now for the honour of England. Fire and behave brave and the French will run.'

The Jacobites once again attempted to put a Catholic Stuart on the British throne during the Jacobite Rising of 1745. The Stuart in rebellion this time was Charles Edward Stuart, Bonnie Prince Charlie, or the Young Pretender. Charles Edward was the son of the Old Pretender, James Francis Edward Stuart, and the grandson of King James II. The rebellion failed and the Jacobites were defeated once and for all at the Battle of Culloden in 1746 by an army led by King George II's son Prince William, Duke of Cumberland, who gained the nickname 'Butcher of Culloden' for his brutality on the battlefield.

King George's son Frederick Louis, born in 1707, was heir to the throne but died prematurely after a freak accident. He was a keen cricketer and it is reported that in 1731 he played for a Surrey XI against a London XI at Kennington Common. Other appearances were documented in the popular press. In 1748 he was hit in the chest by a cricket ball while playing at his summer residence, Cliveden

House, Buckinghamshire. There were medical complications and a burst abscess was the cause of his death in 1751.

As George II had hated his father, he also hated his son Frederick: in a casual aside when he was playing cards he said, 'I have lost my eldest son, but was glad of it.'

George II died at the age of 76 of a heart attack in Kensington Palace, while sitting on the toilet. His death was mourned by few.

GEORGE III

1738–1820, reigned 1760–1820
Son of Frederick, Prince of Wales,
and Augusta of Saxe-Coburg and Gotha

George III was the first monarch since Queen Anne to speak English as a first language. The grandson of George II, he was 22 when he became king. George was proud to be English and in his coronation speech he said: 'Born and bred in this country, I glory in the name Briton.' He never visited his royal house's home of Hanover. But neither, in fact, did he ever visit Wales, Scotland or Ireland – and nor indeed, the north of England.

He married 17-year-old Charlotte Sophia of Mecklenburg-Strelitz two weeks before his coronation – just six hours after he had met her. It was obviously an arranged marriage, and gives a whole new meaning to the phrase whirlwind romance. George and Charlotte led a long, happy and prosaic life of domesticity. They lived at first in a small palace at Kew, but in 1762 George bought Buckingham House, which later became Buckingham Palace. He called it the Queen's House, and many of their children

– nine sons (including two future kings) and six daughters – were born there. 'My quiver is full,' he is reported to have said after the birth of his 15th child, a reference to Psalm 127:6 – 'Happy is the man that hath his quiver full of them (children).'

Domestic virtue was a rare trait in his family, but he was utterly faithful to Charlotte in 57 years of married life. A sense of their closeness is given in Alan Bennett's play and film *The Madness of King George* with Nigel Hawthorne playing George and Helen Mirren playing Charlotte. In the film, they addressed each other affectionately as Mr King and Mrs King.

George was on the throne for 60 years, a reign that would not be exceeded until overtaken by Queen Victoria and then later by Queen Elizabeth II. His reign was great in many senses, and included massive geopolitical changes as well as the changes brought in by the Industrial Revolution. Whether he was a great king was another matter. Unfairly, he is most remembered today for losing the American Colonies and going mad.

If his married life seemed straightforward, George's relations with Parliament were not. He was determined to cut back on some of the power the Whigs had accumulated since 1714. He made John Stuart, Earl of Bute, his prime minister and began replacing Whig politicians with his own men – known as the King's Friends. It did not go down well at Westminster.

Bute resigned after two years and it was not until 1770 that George seemed to have found his man and appointed Lord North as a prime minister he could trust.

⚜ THE AMERICAN REVOLUTION

Thirteen British colonies stretched down the east coast of America from Maine to Georgia. In the 1760s, the colonists resisted British demands for higher taxes and duties to pay for the cost of their defence. 'No taxation without representation' became their famous and effective rallying cry. No one piece of legislation did more damage to British-American relations than the Stamp Act of 1765 which required the colonists to pay a tax on every piece of printed paper they used. They were small amounts of money but this was the first time that Britain had the aim of raising money from levies on the colonies

American radicals saw George III as a tyrant, trying to crush them and deny them their independence. To many Americans, he still is a bogeyman. From the British perspective, the American colonists' demands for more say in their affairs were preposterous. In a response to a petition from the Lord Mayor of London, George III said: 'It is with the utmost astonishment that I find any of my subjects capable of encouraging the rebellious disposition which unhappily exists in some of my colonies in north America.'

In 1770, Lord North's government abolished all the duties, except the one on tea. Three years later, more than 100 protestors dressed as Native Americans boarded a British ship in Boston harbour and threw the cargo of tea overboard (there were 342 chests, weighing 45 tons). This was the Boston Tea Party, one of the most iconic events in American history.

George III wanted to bring the colonists to heel. Lord North's administration agreed, as did most of the House of Commons. But the colonists were becoming more and more resentful of British rule.

Representatives from the colonies met at Philadelphia in 1775 and agreed it was time to break away from Britain. Fighting broke out that year between the British and the colonists in New England.

On 4 July 1776, Congress issued the Declaration of Independence and George Washington was made commander-in-chief of the colonists' army.

DECLARATION OF INDEPENDENCE

The Declaration of Independence, largely written by Thomas Jefferson, was published on 4 July 1776, declaring George III to be 'unfit to be the ruler of a free people'. It starts famously with these words:

> We hold these truths to be self-evident, that all men are created equal; that they are endowed by their Creator with certain unalienable Rights; that among these are Life, Liberty, and the pursuit of Happiness.

The Declaration goes on:

> The history of the present King of Great Britain is a history of repeated injuries and usurpations, all having in direct object the establishment of an absolute Tyranny over these States. To prove this, let Facts be submitted to a candid world.

There then followed an indictment with 27 charges of increasing severity levelled against George III. The Declaration laid out a 'long train of abuses' culminating in absolute tyranny:

> The king is a tyrant, unfit to be the ruler of a free people, deaf to the pleas of justice and humanity. The Congress is forced to proclaim the colonies free and independent states, and the delegates pledge to each other their Lives... Fortunes and... sacred Honor.

King George was not impressed: 'Knavery seems to be so much the striking feature of its [the colonies'] inhabitants that it may not in the end be an evil that they will become aliens to this kingdom.'

The war broadened out as the French joined the colonists, then Spain and in 1780 the Dutch. In 1781, Washington trapped the British at Yorktown, Virginia, and forced a surrender. The war ended in 1784. Five years later, Washington became the first President of the United States of America.

After losing America, George had a difficult time with Parliament and appointed William Pitt the Younger as prime minister in 1785. The 24-year-old son of William Pitt would be prime minister until 1801 and again from 1804 to 1806. Pitt helped George through troubled times. One of the first was in 1788 when George suffered a bout of insanity. He began talking gibberish and it was reported that he talked to a tree in Windsor Great Park thinking that he was addressing the King of Prussia.

Other signs, like frothing at the mouth and bloodshot eyes, suggest he may have been suffering from porphyria, a blood disorder causing mental disturbance. Doctors put him in a straitjacket and his head was blistered so that malignant humours could escape from his brain. But to great popular rejoicing, he recovered from this bout of the illness.

But it returned in 1810 after the death of Princess Amelia, his youngest and favourite daughter. He was in his seventies now, and back in a straitjacket. He never recovered and spent his last years in a padded chamber at Windsor, going blind and deaf at the same time. In the end, he could not recognise his own family.

He was buried in 1820 at St George's Chapel in an enlarged vault that he had ordered. His son George became Prince Regent in 1811 ruling on his father's behalf.

A STAR IS BORN

Sir William Herschel discovered a planet in 1781 and was asked to name it by the Astronomer Royal. He suggested Georgium Sidus, George's Star, in honour of his patron George III who funded the 40-foot telescope that Herschel used. The name was not popular outside Britain, and the planet eventually became known as Uranus.

DID YOU KNOW?

George III was one of the greatest ever book collectors. He started collecting at an early age, and eventually owned 65,000 books as well as assorted maps and charts, pamphlets and manuscripts.

The collection included many rare and priceless editions: a first edition by Caxton of Chaucer's *Canterbury Tales* in 1476; a copy of the Gutenberg Bible; Shakespeare First, Second, Third and Fourth folios; a first edition of *Paradise Lost*. Special rooms housed the books in Buckingham House and the King welcomed scholars of all beliefs and political views to the library.

On his death, his son George IV gave the entire collection to the British Museum. The King's Library is now housed, spectacularly, in a six-storey glass tower at the British Library in London.

GEORGE IV

1762–1830, reigned 1820–1830
Son of George III and Charlotte
Sophia of Mecklenburg-Strelitz

George IV was crowned in July 1821 aged 58 but had already reigned for nine years as Prince Regent when he stood in for his mad father. George IV's drinking habits and sex life were the talk of the time and he appeared to have no inhibitions. His father tried to rein him in, but to no avail and the animosity between father and eldest son followed a well-trodden Hanoverian path. He ran up massive personal debts in his lifetime.

One of his first conquests was an actress called Mary Robinson who was playing Perdita in *The Winter's Tale* at Drury Lane. He pestered her under the name of Florizel, Perdita's lover in the play. The nickname of Florizel stuck with him for a short time, but he was generally known as Prinny (short for Prince of Wales and Prince Regent).

His first marriage to Maria Fitzherbert was annulled for contravening the Royal Marriage Act, which enabled him to marry an 'official' wife chosen for him by Parliament, Caroline of Brunswick. Parliament paid off a large amount of his large debts to encourage him to marry Caroline. George never liked her, and the feeling was mutual. When he was introduced to her, he took a courtier aside and said: 'I am not well; pray get me a glass of brandy.'

He appeared drunk at the wedding and was supported, literally by the sound of it, by the Dukes of Bedford and Roxburghe as he took his vows. According to Caroline, he spent their wedding night completely drunk, passing out in a fireplace before he eventually got into bed with her in the morning. He then proceeded to spend most of their honeymoon intoxicated.

In 1820, after he took the throne, he attempted with the backing of Parliament to divorce her for adultery. At his coronation (which was probably the most spectacular ever staged) he gave the order that all the doors at Westminster Abbey should be locked and she should not be allowed into the ceremony. It is reported that she went round the building hammering in vain on the doors.

George IV's main legacy was buildings. No expense was spared on the Royal Pavilion at Brighton, which stands out for its exotic mix of Indian and Chinese styles. His architect John Nash was responsible for Regent's Park and its elegant terraces and town-houses, and also Regent Street, which was originally built as a new road between the Park and the Regent's home at Carlton House at the end of The Mall.

He was also responsible for Buckingham Palace as we know it today. Originally Buckingham House had been a modest residence – modest that is for kings. But Nash reshaped it and also did major work at Windsor Castle.

During his ten-year reign as king, the Royal Academy of Music was established, the British Museum extended, the National Gallery established, the ban on trade unions lifted, the Metropolitan Police force set up and an act passed in 1829 allowed Catholics to become members of Parliament.

George became grossly overweight well before middle age. He was called the Prince of Whales and was lampooned mercilessly. A cartoon of him – 'A Voluptuary under the Horrors of Digestion' – by James Gilray in 1792 shows a post-prandial, corpulent Prince of Wales almost bursting his breeches, picking his teeth with a fork, surrounded by empty glasses, empty bottles and unpaid bills. George's waist measured 50 inches in 1824, and by 1830, he weighed more than 20 stones. From 1824 onwards, he suffered badly from gout and to relieve the pain, he took heavier and heavier doses of laudanum.

His afflictions did not seem to affect his appetite. The Duke of Wellington wrote to a friend in 1830 describing a breakfast King George had eaten the day before:

> He had a Pigeon and Beefsteak Pie, of which he ate two pigeons and three beefsteaks. Three parts of a Bottle of Moselle, a Glass of Dry Champagne, two glasses of Port and a Glass of Brandy... he had taken laudanum the night before and again before this breakfast.

George grew ever more reclusive as he aged, and died of a heart attack at Windsor Castle in 1830. His obituary in *The Times* was cruel:

> There was never an individual less regretted by his fellow creatures than this deceased King [...] If he ever had a friend, a devoted friend from any rank of life, we protest that the name of him or her never reached us.

WILLIAM IV

1765–1837, reigned 1830–1837
Son of George III and Charlotte
Sophia of Mecklenburg-Strelitz

William IV was the third son of George III and as such did not expect to ever succeed to the throne. George IV had only one daughter, Princess Charlotte, who died in childbirth in 1817 and William's elder brother Frederick, Duke of York, died in 1827.

William was the oldest monarch to take the English throne – he was 65. He was awakened and turfed out of bed at 6 a.m. to be told that his brother George IV had died and that he was now King William IV of the United Kingdom of Great Britain and Ireland and Hanover. He said that he had always wanted to sleep with a queen – and with that, went quickly back upstairs to bed to be with his Adelaide.

He had gone to sea when he was 13 and was widely known as the Sailor King. He worked his way up through the ranks of the Royal Navy to take command of his own ship, HMS *Pegasus*, in 1786. He served under Lord Nelson in the West Indies and the two became great friends. In 1789, he was promoted to rear-admiral in charge of HMS *Valiant*, when he was made Duke of Clarence, but retired from active service the following year. He was made admiral in 1798, but the rank was in name only, as was the title of Admiral of the Fleet granted in 1811.

He lived in unmarried happiness from 1791 to 1811 with an actress Mrs Dorothea Jordan and together they had ten illegitimate children known as the Fitzclarences. William needed a legitimate heir and in 1818, he married a German princess, Adelaide of Saxe-Meiningen. They had two daughters, but both died in infancy.

William was much more frugal than his brother had been and this helped to make him a popular king; he insisted on a coronation that cost a tenth of his brother's. He did not like fuss and often used his family name William Guelph to hide his identity

The seven years of his reign saw some of the most important constitutional and political battles of the century, but William, albeit in a grudging way, decided to steer clear of politics. He understood the theory and practice of the more limited monarchy, and once said: 'I have my view of things, and I tell them to my ministers. If they do not adopt them, I cannot help it. I have done my duty.'

 ## SILLY BILLY, THE SHARP-TONGUED KING

William was wont to speak his mind and he could sometimes lack tact, which led to his other nickname Silly Billy. The stories endeared him to the people.

One day when William was being shown around the Royal Academy, the president of the RA pointed out a portrait of Admiral Napier. William hated Napier, and exploded: 'Capt Napier may be damn'd sir! And you may be damn'd too, sir, and if the Queen was not here, sir, I would kick you downstairs.'

Once when he was dining, he espied King Leopold of the Belgians sipping water. William exploded again: 'God damn it, why don't you drink wine? I never let anybody drink water at my table.'

One of his pet hates was the Duchess of Kent, widow of his brother Edward and mother of the future Queen Victoria. He wanted Victoria to be 18 before she succeeded to the throne to prevent the duchess becoming Regent. He bluntly told her:

> I trust to God that my life may be spared for nine months longer […] I should then have the satisfaction of leaving the exercise of the Royal authority to the personal authority of that young lady, heiress presumptive to the Crown, and not in the hands of a person now near me, who is surrounded by evil advisers and is herself incompetent to act with propriety in the situation in which she would be placed. [He got his wish.]

Queen Victoria was generous in her praise for her uncle. 'Whatever his faults may have been... he was not only zealous but most conscientious in the discharge of his duties as king. He had a truly kind heart and was anxious to do what was right.'

He died of pneumonia and cirrhosis weeks after Victoria's 18th birthday in 1837; his last words to his wife, Adelaide, at his bedside were: 'Bear up! Oh come – bear up, bear up!'

DID YOU KNOW?

There is no memorial to Adelaide in the UK, but she is well remembered in Australia: the city of Adelaide was named in her honour in 1836.

VICTORIA

1819–1901, reigned 1837–1901
Daughter of Edward, Duke of Kent,
and Victoria of Saxe-Coburg-Saalfeld

Alexandrina Victoria, to give the princess her full name, was born in Kensington Palace in 1819, and acceded to the throne on the death of her uncle, William IV, in 1837. She was just 18.

In a speech in the Privy Council on her day of accession, June 20, 1837, she said:

> I place my firm reliance upon the wisdom of Parliament and upon the loyalty and affection of my People. Educated in England under the tender and enlightened care of a most affectionate Mother I have learned from my Infancy to respect and love the Constitution of my native Country.

The grace and dignity of these words belied her age and bode well for the future.

Her tutor had corrected the Germanic accent, and she went on progresses around the country in homage to Queen Elizabeth I. The prime minister Lord Melbourne played a quasi-paternal role – in fact in her diary of the coronation day, Victoria said: 'Lord Melbourne gave me such a kind & I may say, fatherly look.'

Victoria was determined to restore the reputation of the monarchy and an early chance came in her first major public engagement as monarch – her coronation in June 1838. It was reported that 400,000 people lined the route from St James's Palace to Westminster Abbey. That was a gross underestimate according to Victoria – she wrote in her journal: 'There were millions of my loyal subjects, assembled in every spot, to witness the Procession.'

The *Globe* newspaper reported:

> Her Majesty's carriages and attendants, in twelve carriages, each drawn by six beautiful bays, were the subject of much admiration [...] Her Majesty's State Carriage approached – this was the signal for the kindliest and most affectionate demonstrations, and a shout, echoed and re-echoed along St James's Street and Pall Mall – deep, fervent and enthusiastic – was sent up from the immense assemblage.

Victoria was an attractive woman. She spoke German, French and Italian, painted, and kept a detailed and well-written journal. She also had a strong character: though she was only five foot tall, she would not be ordered around by anyone.

Victoria first met her cousin, Prince Albert of Saxe-Coburg and Gotha, in 1836 and they got on well. Victoria thought he was 'extremely good-looking'. She wrote in her journal: 'He is perfection, perfection in every way – in beauty, in everything. Oh how I adore and love him... It was with some emotion that I beheld Albert, who is beautiful.'

Victoria wrote to King Leopold I of the Belgians, who seems to have played the role of royal matchmaker:

> I must thank you, my beloved Uncle, for the prospect of great happiness, you have contributed to give me, in the person of dear Albert. Allow me, then, my dearest Uncle, to tell you how delighted I am with him, and how

much I like him in every way. He possesses every quality that could be desired to render me perfectly happy. He is so sensible, so kind, and so good, and so amiable too. He has besides, the most pleasing and delightful exterior and appearance you can possibly see.

On their second meeting in 1839, she decided it really was true love (it clearly was) and five days after he arrived in England, she asked Albert to marry her. Protocol demanded that the Queen did the proposing. They were engaged in October 1839 and married at the Chapel Royal at St James's Palace in February 1840.

Albert wrote to Victoria in 1839: 'Even in my dreams I never imagined that I should find so much love on earth. How that moment shines for me when I was close to you, but with your hand in mine.'

Parliament did not want to give him the title of king and so Victoria gave him the title of Prince Consort and he assisted the Queen and was her trusted principal adviser in affairs of state throughout their marriage.

CHRISTMAS TRADITIONS

Victoria and Albert popularised the way Christmas came to be celebrated in Britain. Christmas trees and Christmas cards were already German traditions (Albert was German, and Victoria's mother was German) but for most British people, having a tree in the house was unheard of. A branch of holly or mistletoe or yew might be brought into the house, but that was it.

Albert imported several spruce trees from Germany and the tradition caught on with the masses after engravings of the family in front of a big Christmas tree appeared in journals like the *Illustrated London News* in the 1840s.

Later in Victoria's reign, Christmas cards could be printed quite cheaply, and with postage at a halfpenny 11.5 million were sold in 1880. The commercialisation of Christmas had begun.

THE VICTORIA CROSS

The Victoria Cross is the highest award for gallantry in action with the enemy. The inscription on the medal, chosen by the Queen herself, is 'For Valour'. It emerged from the Crimean War as a bravery award for the common soldier. Previously, only senior officers had been awarded medals. MPs backed the idea and the proposal had a major and important supporter, Prince Albert. He won the backing of his wife, and he himself suggested the name – the Victoria Cross. It was first awarded in 1856.

The bronze for the medals came from a captured Chinese-made cannon used by the Russians at Sebastopol during the Crimean War. What is left today of the metal is kept at an army base in Shropshire – there is only enough left now for 80 more medals.

Since its inception, more than 1,350 Victoria Crosses have been awarded.

⚜ THE GREAT EXHIBITION

The Great Exhibition of the Works of Industry of All Nations was an international expo in Hyde Park, London, from May to October 1851.

It was the first-ever international exhibition of manufactured products and Prince Albert was a prime mover: he saw it as a festival of 'peace and love' (makes it sound a bit like Glastonbury).

It was sometimes referred to as the Crystal Palace Exhibition in reference to the temporary structure in which it was held. The specially built 'crystal palace' used 4,500 tons of iron framework holding close to 300,000 panes of glass. At almost 20 metres high, it was big enough to contain some of the park's trees. It stretched over an area of 20 acres.

The Crystal Palace itself was adjudged to be an enormous success, considered an architectural marvel and an engineering triumph that highlighted the importance of the Exhibition itself. The building was later moved to South London, to the area that now bears its name in fact, where it burnt down in 1936.

The exhibits included almost every marvel of the Victorian age, including pottery, porcelain, ironwork, furniture, perfumes, pianos, firearms, fabrics, steam hammers, hydraulic presses and even the odd house or two.

Queen Victoria opened the exhibition and wrote in her journal for 1 May 1851: 'This day is one of the greatest and most glorious of our lives [...] It is a day which makes my heart swell with thankfulness.'

There were doubters – *The Times* thought Hyde Park was being transformed into 'something between Wolverhampton and the Greenwich Fair'. But it soon caught the popular imagination. More than 6 million people visited the Exhibition, almost one-third of the total population. Victoria visited the Exhibition with her family 13 times.

Albert raised most of the money for the event, which made a surplus of £186,000. This was used to buy 87 acres of land in South Kensington to the south of the Exhibition stretching from Kensington Gore to the Cromwell Road and additionally to finance the founding of the Victoria and Albert Museum, the Natural History Museum, the Science Museum, the Royal College of Art, the Royal College of Music, Imperial College and the Royal Albert Hall. The Albert Memorial opposite the Albert Hall, a highly ornate Gothic-style monument, has Prince Albert holding the catalogue for the Great Exhibition.

⚜ AFTER ALBERT

After twenty-one years of happy marriage, tragedy struck in 1861 when Albert contracted typhoid as a result of a fever when he was caught in a storm. He died aged 42. Queen Victoria was overwhelmed by grief at the loss of her beloved husband. She wrote to King Leopold a week after Albert died:

> To be cut off in the prime of life – to see our pure happy, quiet domestic life, which alone enabled me to bear my much disliked position, cut off at 42 – when I had hoped with such instinctive certainty that God never would part us, and would let us grow old together – is too awful, too cruel.

Victoria sank into a deep depression following Albert's death, and retreated from public view for many years. She wore black for the rest of her life – more than 40 years. She rarely appeared in public until the late 1860s; although she never neglected her official correspondence, and continued to give audiences to her ministers and official visitors, she was reluctant to resume a full public life.

John Brown, a ghillie in charge of the stables at Balmoral, became the unlikely person to cheer up Victoria. The royal doctor had said that exercise would help the Queen, and suggested that Brown take the Queen out riding. He made a favourable impression on her and always led her pony when she went riding. In 1858, Albert had promoted him to Head Servant in Scotland, which, for a servant, was an exalted position.

When Albert died, the 6-foot-tall Brown was brought south from his post at Balmoral to become Victoria's personal groom at Osborne and he became increasingly important to the Queen, who became to rely on him for his loyalty and no-nonsense ways.

Victoria began to address Brown as 'darling' in her letters to him, and rumours began to fly: they were having an affair; Victoria had a child by him; they were married. Only one thing is certain – they clearly had a very, very close relationship. John Brown is best remembered today thanks to the acclaimed 1997 film *Mrs Brown*, starring Dame Judi Dench and Billy Connolly. He died aged 56 at Windsor Castle in 1883.

 A ROYAL RETREAT

Victoria and Albert built Osborne House at East Cowes on the Isle of Wight from 1845 to 1851 in an attempt to get away from the pressures of London. Albert designed it on the lines of an Italian renaissance palazzo. Money from the sale of the Brighton Pavilion helped to pay for it.

The royal family stayed at Osborne for lengthy periods each year: in the spring for Victoria's birthday; in the summer; and just before Christmas.

In a break from tradition, Victoria and Albert allowed photographers and painters to capture their family in the grounds and in the house, partly for their own enjoyment and partly to show the nation what a happy and devoted family they were.

In 1876, as a tribute to Queen Victoria, the Government House of the colony (now state) of Victoria, Australia, was built as a copy of Osborne House.

Prince Albert gave the royal children a wonderful present at Osborne in 1854 – the Swiss Cottage, which was a two-storey super-Wendy House complete with kitchen and dining room, designed for children to feel at home.

There were nine little gardens outside the cottage (one for each of Victoria and Albert's nine little children), marked out and named. The children could grow whatever they wanted in their little vegetable patch and Albert would buy garden produce from them to use at the House.

⚜ THE LITTLE LADY IN BLACK

In the 1870s Victoria began to appear more regularly in public and she regained a renewed sense of purpose encouraged by Benjamin Disraeli, who knew how to encourage her and flatter her. In 1876, he made her Empress of India: he described India as 'the jewel in her crown'.

The little lady in black had become a legend and the figurehead of the nation: her reign caught the public mood. She was strong willed and her relations with her prime ministers ranged from the affectionate (Melbourne and Disraeli) to the stormy (Peel, Palmerston and Gladstone). Victoria once complained that Gladstone 'always addresses me as if I were a public meeting'.

The British Empire was at the height of its power in the 1870s and the Queen nominally ruled over 450 million people, one quarter of the world's population and approximately one quarter of the world's landmass. Stretching from Canada to the Caribbean, Africa, India, Australia and New Zealand, it was proudly said that the sun never set on the British Empire.

Victoria's Golden Jubilee in 1887 was the focus of national pride both in Britain and throughout the British Empire. Her carriage in procession to Westminster Abbey was followed by 30 of her sons, sons-in-law and grandsons from all over Europe.

The Diamond Jubilee in 1897 was an even bigger national patriotic celebration, and 50,000 soldiers from all over the world were involved. In her journal, the Queen wrote:

> No one ever, I believe, has met with such an ovation as was given to me, passing through those six miles of streets [...] The cheering was quite deafening & every face seemed to be filled with real joy. I was much moved and gratified.

 FLORENCE NIGHTINGALE

In 1856, Queen Victoria awarded Florence Nightingale a brooch for her services in the Crimean war. The brooch was a sign of royal appreciation at a time when suitable decorations for female civilians did not exist. Known as the Nightingale Jewel, and designed with the supervision of Prince Albert, it is engraved with a dedication from the Queen: 'To Miss Florence Nightingale, as a mark of esteem and gratitude for her devotion towards the Queen's brave soldiers, from Victoria R. 1855.'

In a letter to the nurse, the Queen wrote: 'It will be a very great satisfaction to me, when you return at last to these shores, to make the acquaintance of one who has set so bright an example to our sex.'

⚜ VICTORIA AND ALBERT'S CHILDREN

Queen Victoria and Prince Albert had nine children: four boys and five girls. The oldest six children were born between 1840 and 1848.

1. Victoria, Princess Royal (1840–1901)

As the eldest daughter, Victoria was given the title Princess Royal. In 1858, she married Prince Frederick of Prussia and became Empress of Germany when he succeeded his father as Emperor Frederick III. They had eight children, the oldest Wilhelm becoming Emperor Wilhelm II (the Kaiser) on the death of his father in 1888. That's Kaiser Bill.

2. Albert Edward, Prince of Wales (1841–1910)

He became Prince of Wales as he was heir apparent to the throne. He married Princess Alexandra of Denmark at Windsor in 1863 and succeeded to the throne as Edward VII in 1901 when Queen Victoria died. He died in 1910.

3. Alice (1843–1878)

Married Prince Louis of Hesse-Darmstadt in 1862 and was given the grand title of Grand Duchess of Hesse-Darmstadt.

They had seven children. Their daughter Alexandra became the most famous of their offspring as Tsarina of Russia, married to Nicholas II of Russia, murdered with her husband and their five children during the Russian Revolution.

4. Alfred (1844–1900)

The Duke of Edinburgh and Saxe-Coburg and Gotha. He married Princess Marie Alexandrovna, Grand Duchess of Russia, at St Petersburg in 1874.

5. Helena (1846–1923)
She married Prince Christian of Schleswig-Holstein in 1866 and was known as Princess Helena of Schleswig-Holstein.

6. Louise (1848–1939)
She married the Marquess of Lorne in 1871 and on his death, took the title Dowager, Duchess of Argyll. She was a talented sculptor and a statue by her of Queen Victoria is in Kensington Gardens.

7. Arthur (1850–1942)
Duke of Connaught, he married Princess Louise Margaret of Prussia in 1879.

8. Leopold (1853–1884)
Duke of Albany, he married Princess Helena of Waldeck and Pyrmont. Their daughter Princess Alice was Queen Victoria's oldest surviving grandchild until her death in 1981.

9. Beatrice (1857–1944)
She married Prince Henry of Battenburg and held the title of Princess Beatrice of Battenburg. Henry died of a fever while serving with the British Army in 1896 and Beatrice, a widow at 38, became very close to her mother.

Only one of Victoria's children, Louise, married a British citizen. The other eight of the children sat on the thrones of Europe: Great Britain, Prussia, Greece, Romania, Russia, Norway, Sweden and Spain.

On 22 January 1901, Queen Victoria, who had become known as the 'Grandmother of Europe', died at Osborne, reportedly in the arms of her oldest and favourite grandchild, Wilhelm, Kaiser Bill-to-be. Her funeral was held at St George's Chapel,

Windsor, and she was buried in Frogmore Mausoleum next to her husband, Prince Albert.

 ## WHAT'S IN A NAME?

More places and streets have been named after Victoria than any other British monarch. Victoria must be the most used first name in the world. The *London A–Z* has 40 entries for Victoria Road alone, and myriads more: Victoria Avenue, Close, Court, Crescent, Grove, Lane, Mansions, Mews, Street, Terrace. There are many Queen's Roads as well; there is no proof, but it is likely that most of them will refer to Queen Victoria.

In London, there is the Victoria and Albert museum, Victoria Embankment, Victoria Park, Victoria Station (rail and coach) and the Royal Victoria Dock.

Manchester has a Victoria railway station; Newcastle the Royal Victoria Infirmary; and Belfast, Queen's University and the Royal Victoria Hospital.

Two states in Australia are named after her: The state of Queensland, and the state of Victoria, as well as the Great Victoria Desert, Lake Alexandrina (South Australia), Queen's College, Melbourne, and Queen Victoria Hospital, Melbourne.

In Canada there is the Royal Victoria Hospital, Montreal; Victoria Bridge, Montreal; Queen's University, Kingston; Victoria University, Toronto; Victoria, the capital of British Columbia; Regina, Saskatchewan; Victoria, Newfoundland; and Victoriaville, Quebec.

The famous explorer David Livingstone named the Victoria Falls after the Queen in 1855. The first European to set eyes on the largest lake in Africa was British explorer John Speke in 1858 on an expedition to find the source of the Nile. He named the lake Victoria in honour of the Queen.

In New Zealand just outside Wellington, Mount Victoria (196m) is physically linked by a ridge to Mount Albert.

There was clearly a royalist hotspot in a part of Cheshire in the 1870s. Northwich Victoria football club was founded in 1874 and three years later, nearby Crewe took the name Alexandra after the Princess of Wales, wife of the future Edward VII.

Last but not least, the most famous pub in Britain is named after her – the Queen Vic.

HOUSE OF SAXE-COBURG AND GOTHA

EDWARD VII

1841–1910, reigned 1901–1910
Son of Queen Victoria and Prince
Albert of Saxe-Coburg and Gotha

Albert Edward, the eldest son of Victoria and Albert, was universally known as Bertie. He had to wait until he was almost 60 to succeed to the throne, which led almost inevitably to a life that bordered at times on the dissolute. His relations with his parents were not good. He once said: 'I don't mind praying to the Eternal Father, but I must be the only man in the country afflicted with an Eternal Mother.'

His mother's view of him was hardly more complimentary – she thought he was stupid. Victoria told her daughter Alice: 'He does nothing... He shows more and more how totally totally unfit he is for ever becoming King.' In her journal, she confided, 'Oh that boy. Much as I pity him, I never can, or shall, look at him without a shudder.' And his father took a similar critical line: 'He is lively, quick and sharp when his mind is set on anything, which is seldom.'

Edward married Princess Alexandra, elder daughter of King Christian IX of Denmark, in 1863. She was beautiful and elegant and they had six children in seven years, one of whom was to reign as George V. Despite his seemingly happy marriage and home life, Bertie took many mistresses, at least 13 according to one account. One of his nicknames, well-earned, during his reign was 'Edward the Caresser'. Alexandra showed much patience, saying once: 'He always loved me the best.' Bertie said Alexandra was his 'Brood mare... The others are my hacks'.

He seemed particularly fond of actresses and society beauties, such as Lillie Langtree and Sarah Bernhardt, the Countess of Warwick, and Mrs Alice Keppel, who was his favourite. The latter was married to George Keppel, son of the 7th Earl of Albermarle in 1891, and both of them embarked on a series of affairs, which seemed to be de rigueur in their circle at the time.

Alice met the Prince of Wales in 1898 when she was 29 and he was 56, and she became his close confidante. She was at the King's side at the biggest events of the London season, at Cowes and Ascot, as well as dinner parties on the royal yacht and shooting parties at Sandringham.

Her advice to would-be royal mistresses was simple: 'Curtsey first, then leap into bed.' Edward and Alice were very close; her children played with the King – one of them called him Kingy.

In a strange repeat of history, Alice's great-granddaughter Camilla Parker Bowles would become the mistress of another Prince of Wales, Charles, and indeed marry him.

Edward spent a large part of his time, especially before he became king, in the pursuit of pleasure. He liked gambling, playing cards, shooting and hunting, and was a successful racehorse owner – he won the Derby three times and the Grand National once.

Nothing was done to prepare him for his future role as king and not until he was a grandfather himself would Victoria allow him access to Cabinet papers.

Eating was also one of his passions: he ate five meals every day including a 12-course dinner. His waistline ballooned to 48 inches and led to another nickname: Tum Tum. He often left undone the bottom button of his waistcoat; this was immediately adjudged to be a regal fashion statement, and has been the correct way to wear a waistcoat ever since.

It is also said that he 'invented' trouser turn-ups. He used to roll up his trousers in bad weather to stop his trousers becoming muddied. At the turn of the 20th century, he incorporated the turn-up in his tailored trousers. It quickly became fashionable.

Edward VII proved to be a popular king, and was a good diplomat and an effective ambassador for the nation. He carefully fostered relationships with other countries and was largely responsible for the Entente Cordiale with France.

On one of his many trips to Paris, the Prince of Wales was greeted one night at the Moulin Rouge by a dancer who obviously knew him well. 'Hello, Wales,' she shouted: '*Est-ce que tu vas payer mon champagne?*' '*Oui,*' he said, and proceeded to buy champagne for the dancers and all the members of the orchestra.

He smoked 20 cigarettes a day, which was probably par for the course in those days, but he also smoked 12 'massive' cigars. When he became king, he famously ended the ban on smoking that Queen Victoria had enforced at court with the words, immortal in cigar history (there is such a thing), 'Gentlemen, you may smoke.' A brand of cigars was named after him and King Edward Cigars became at one time the best-selling brand in the world and they are still big sellers today. More mundanely, he gave his name to a new type of potato – the now ubiquitous King Edward – which was introduced into the UK in the year of his coronation, 1902.

Prince Albert had bought the Sandringham estate in Norfolk just before he died as a country house for the Prince and Princess of Wales in an attempt to wean Bertie away from the enticing pleasures of London.

The royal couple loved the house and extended it into a 270-room Jacobean-style residence. The Prince bred his racehorses and organised successful shooting parties there.

Alexandra kept the main house until she died in 1925. Sandringham became a much loved royal family retreat and both George V and VI died there and members of the present Royal Family are very happy still to use it as a home from home.

 ROYAL ICING

Before he was king, Edward and his son George V-to-be can lay claim to being the first members of the royal family to play ice hockey.

The modern game had started in Canada, and in 1895 during a very severe winter, a 'Buckingham Palace Team' played a 'Lord Stanley Team' made up of Anglo-Canadians.

The match was played in January on the lake at the Palace which had iced over.

It was reported that 'the visiting side scored numerous goals to the single one of the Palace side'. That's a polite way of saying that the royal team was thrashed.

Despite the efforts of his courtiers to keep any indiscretions out of the public gaze, the prince was forced on two occasions to give evidence in court.

In 1870, an MP, Sir Charles Mordaunt, brought a divorce petition against his wife on the grounds of adultery with two of the Prince of Wales's friends. Lady Mordaunt admitted her adultery but then implicated Bertie.

Edward's denial in court of Lady Mordaunt's allegations was accepted. The evidence, however, proved that the prince had visited the lady on a number of occasions in the afternoon when her husband was away in the House of Commons and he had been alone with her. He got the benefit of the doubt, his behaviour being judged indiscreet but not improper...

Twenty years later Edward was back in court. He was staying in Yorkshire when visiting the Doncaster St Leger race meeting and in the evening, the guests played a game of baccarat, which was illegal. One of the guests, a colonel, was accused of cheating. Edward tried to keep the matter private, but the colonel sued some of the players for slander, and at the trial, the prince was subpoenaed as a witness.

Public opinion was scandalised: first that the prince was playing an illegal card game, and second that, as Field Marshall in the Army, he had committed an offence under military rules by not reporting the colonel to his superior officer.

On his deathbed at Buckingham Palace in 1910, Edward muttered: 'I shall not give in. I shall work to the end.' In a touching gesture, Queen Alexandra sent for Mrs Keppel to allow her to say a last goodbye to the King. She held his hand at the end.

THE HOUSE OF
WINDSOR

(SAXE-COBURG AND GOTHA
UNTIL 1917)

GEORGE V

1865–1936, reigned 1910–1936
Son of Edward VII and Princess
Alexandra of Denmark

Prince George Frederick Ernest Albert of Saxe-Coburg and Gotha was born in 1865, the second son of the Prince and Princess of Wales.

He was sent with his elder brother Albert Victor (known to his family as 'Eddy') as a teenager to Naval College at Dartmouth and despite being the youngest cadet, he emerged from the tough regime with credit. George began a career as a naval officer, enjoying the strict training and the regimented life and in 1889 took command of a torpedo boat.

But George's life was to turn upside down in 1892 when his brother, the heir apparent, died of pneumonia. Only a few weeks before, Eddy had become betrothed to Princess Mary of Teck. George, who had never expected to become heir to the throne, was created Duke of York and sat in the House of Lords.

Some commentators have said that Eddy's death was fortuitous for the monarchy. He had learning difficulties – although they weren't called that then – and could have caused the monarchy serious problems.

George's grandmother Queen Victoria was still very much in charge, and she decided that George should marry Eddy's fiancée Princess Mary of Teck. Everybody obeyed the Queen, and their marriage developed into a happy one.

Princess Mary, who was a great-granddaughter of George III, was born in Kensington Palace in the same room as Victoria. She had the advantage of being both royal and English, and beautiful, intelligent and serious to boot. They were married in 1893. So began 42 years of wedded bliss.

As the new Prince and Princess of Wales in 1901, they set off on a tour of the Empire which was to take in Australia, New Zealand, South Africa and Canada, covering 45,000 miles, and involving shaking hands with 25,000 people. In 1911, the royal couple, now King George and Queen Mary, went to Delhi to be crowned Emperor and Empress of India. It was the ceremonial high point of the empire and George was acclaimed as the most important royal person on earth.

The outbreak of the First World War four years after he became king signalled an uncomfortable time, both for the country and himself personally. Many of his closest relations were Germans: he had 50 first cousins, one of whom was the Emperor of Germany himself, Kaiser Wilhelm II, better known in Britain as Kaiser Bill.

George visited the front to boost the morale of the troops and paid numerous visits to factories and hospitals at home. In 1915 while inspecting troops on the Western Front, he was thrown from his horse after it reared up in fright, breaking his pelvis. He still presented medals from his sick bed.

With the war raging, George took on the problem of his German family name, Saxe-Coburg and Gotha, which had come to the royal family in 1840 when Queen Victoria married Prince Albert, son of Ernst, Duke of Saxe-Coburg and Gotha. Victoria remained a member of the House of Hanover. Anti-German feeling and public unrest was rising across Britain during the First World War, and anybody with a German name, or a German-sounding one, was a possible target. It was reported that owners of dachshunds and Bechstein pianos were attacked.

In this climate, George thought it prudent in 1917 to change the name of the Royal House to something that sounded more English. It is not quite clear why it took the royal family so long to come to this decision – among all the other things that were going on at the time, London was being bombed by the Kaiser's Gotha aeroplanes.

On 18 July 1917, there was a royal proclamation in *The Times* under the headline:

WINDSOR. THE KING'S NAME.
ALL GERMAN TITLES DROPPED.

The King has been pleased to declare his determination respecting the name of his House and family, and the discontinuance of all German titles. As regards the name of his House and family, the King's determination is that it shall henceforth be known as of Windsor.

Windsor was the brainchild of King George's private secretary Lord Stamfordham. It was a quite brilliant master stroke.

This elicited a very rare joke from Wilhelm II. On hearing of the name change, he said he was looking forward to a new production of *The Merry Wives of Saxe-Coburg and Gotha*.

Another of George's cousins was Tsar Nicholas II, Emperor of Russia. He was offered asylum by George but that offer was quickly withdrawn. The King was criticised for not going to the aid of the Russian royal family but he had real worries about revolution at home. Tsar Nicholas and his wife and five children were murdered by the Bolsheviks on 16 July 1918.

DID YOU KNOW?

The clocks at Sandringham ran 30 minutes ahead of GMT from 1901 until 1936. This started with Edward VII – it was not for the benefit of his wife, Alexandra, who was famous for being late, but rather a groundbreaking move to save daylight hours, especially in the evening, for hunting in the winter. It was also introduced at Windsor and Balmoral. The custom was abolished when George V died in 1935. It was never restarted.

⚜ PHILATELY

George V amassed a massive collection of stamps from Great Britain and the Empire. There are almost 20,000 pages in his albums and he had the pre-eminent collection in the world. It was said that every British and Empire stamp ever issued was in the collection, which is now held in the Royal Philately Collection at St James's Palace.

He recognised rarity and made every effort to obtain the rarest stamps at the first possible opportunity. By 1904 he had acquired both the penny and two penny post office Mauritius, 1847 – the first stamps issued by a colonial post office and probably the most prized stamps that any collector could wish to acquire. The unused 2*d* stamp was bought at auction for a record price of £1,450. A courtier asked George if he had seen that 'some damned fool had paid as much as £1,400 for one stamp'. 'Yes,' came the reply: 'I was that damned fool!'

It should be pointed out that philately becomes a bit easier and certainly more personal if the only people pictured on the stamps you are collecting are your grandmother, your father and yourself.

 FOOTBALL

George V discovered football and also what football could do for him. He presented the FA Cup in 1921 to Tottenham who beat Wolves in front of 73,000 spectators at Stamford Bridge. George, obviously worried about the spread of Communism and the reaction of the working people to the royal family, wrote to his mother: 'They sang the National Anthem and cheered tremendously. No Bolsheviks there...' He presented the Cup at the famous White Horse Cup Final in 1923 between Bolton and West Ham, the first final played at the newly built Wembley Stadium. Thousands of fans surged on to the pitch and the policeman on the white horse tried to keep order. It was estimated that close to 300,000 people were in the stadium – the official attendance was a mere 126,047.

King George V was surprised by the success of his Silver Jubilee year in 1935. On his way back to Buckingham Palace in the carriage from St Paul's, he said to Queen Mary, 'I believe they really like me.' But he saw the danger signals ahead for his son and heir, the Prince of Wales: 'After I'm gone, the boy will ruin himself in 12 months,' he said to the Archbishop of Canterbury.

His health had been deteriorating for some time: he had bronchial problems and was a heavy smoker. In January 1936 at Sandringham, his doctor gave the King fatal doses of morphine and cocaine to assure a painless death, but also to hasten the end to ensure that the news of the King's death would appear in the quality morning newspapers rather than the evening papers.

Lord Dawson wrote: 'The King's life is moving peacefully toward its close.' Death came less than an hour after the injections. The doctor phoned his wife in London to ask that she 'advise *The Times* to hold back publication'. The headline the next morning read, 'A Peaceful Ending at Midnight'.

CHRISTMAS RADIO BROADCAST

George V delivered the first Christmas radio broadcast in 1932 and it has become an important part of Christmas Day.

The original idea for a broadcast speech by the monarch was suggested by Sir John Reith, founder of the BBC, to inaugurate the Empire Service (now the BBC World Service).

The King was originally wary about the project, but was reassured by a visit to the BBC in the summer of 1932 and agreed to take part.

The transmission involved major logistical problems. Two rooms at Sandringham were converted into 'studios' and the microphones connected through post office landlines to Broadcasting House in London. From there connection was made to BBC Home Service transmitters and to the Empire Broadcasting Station at Daventry with its six short-wave transmitters.

The time chosen for the broadcast was 3pm – the optimum time for reaching most of the countries in the Empire from short-wave transmitters in Britain. On the day, the broadcast started at 3.05pm.

The text was written by Rudyard Kipling and began: 'I speak now from my home and from my heart to you all; to men and women so cut off by the snows, the desert, or the sea, that only voices out of the air can reach them… '

The broadcast made a big impression and attracted a massive audience for its time of 20 million. George V made a broadcast every Christmas until his death in 1936.

EDWARD VIII

1894–1972, reigned Jan-Dec 1936
Son of George V and Mary of Teck

The future King Edward VIII was born at White Lodge, Richmond, the home of his maternal grandparents, the Duke and Duchess of Teck and was christened Edward Albert Christian George Andrew Patrick David in July 1894 by the Archbishop of Canterbury.

The names were chosen in honour of Edward's late uncle Edward; Albert was included at the behest of Queen Victoria for her late husband; Christian after his great-grandfather King Christian IX of Denmark; and the last four names – George, Andrew, Patrick and David – are the patron saints of England, Scotland, Ireland and Wales. He was known to his family and close friends as David.

The well-established pattern of the sour relationship between father and son that had dogged the House of Hanover was soon in evidence. George V's views on childcare were somewhat Neanderthal: 'My father was frightened of his mother, I was frightened of my father and I am damned well going to see to it that my children are frightened of me.' Well, they were.

Edward and his father were polar opposites. Their qualities were a mirror-image of each other's. Edward was charming, approachable and emotional. He hated ceremony and convention – he was a modern, 20th-century boy. His father was not.

After Naval College at Osborne and the Royal Naval College at Dartmouth, Edward attended Magdalen College, Oxford, for two years. He was invested as Prince of Wales at Caernarfon

Castle in July 1911 in a special ceremony that David Lloyd George had created in the style of a Welsh pageant. Lloyd George coached Edward to speak a few words in Welsh.

Edward held a commission in the Grenadier Guards during the First World War but was not allowed to go anywhere near the front despite a personal appeal to Lord Kitchener. Assignments to safe positions on the Italian front troubled him, causing him to say: 'What difference does it make if I am killed? The king has three other sons!'

George V and Mary hoped that he would settle down and marry, but it soon became clear that the Prince of Wales was not interested in the type of girl of which his parents would approve. He had a number of affairs, most notably a passionate relationship with Thelma, Lady Furness and then a five-year affair with Mrs Freda Dudley Ward, wife of a Liberal MP, writing to her at least once a day wherever he was in the world. Eagle-eyed *Downton Abbey* fans saw Mrs Dudley Ward's character make an appearance in the 2013 Christmas special.

Between 1919 and 1935 he made 13 tours, visiting much of the British Empire, and acted as something like a goodwill ambassador. He also visited the United States: he loved Americans and they loved him. He was at the centre of a glittering circle of socialites and was the poster boy of his age.

Edward was a dominant figure in the newsreels after the time. Audiences saw him on his numerous visits to industrial areas and the inner cities, touring factories, visiting housing estates, opening hospitals and inspecting lines of ex-servicemen in Britain and France.

He was a popular Prince of Wales. During the Depression he visited the worst-hit areas and saw for himself the poverty and hardship. 'Something must be done,' he said during a visit to the abandoned Dowlais steelworks near Merthyr Tydfil on a tour of the South Wales mining valleys. But it wasn't clear what.

His friends noticed that two characteristics became stronger as he became older – his vanity and his hatred of publicity. He could not see that the attention being paid to him was based as much on his position as for any innate personal gifts of personality, and this made him more vain than he already was.

In a desire to get away from the world of publicity, he moved to Fort Belvedere near Sunningdale. It was in these quiet surroundings that his relationship with Mrs Wallis Simpson would flourish. He first met Wallis Simpson in 1931, one of a circle of fashionable friends that the prince found entertaining. She had been twice married, and her second husband, Ernest Simpson, an American businessman, had served with the British forces in the war. Edward seemed to be mesmerised by her, and wrote hundreds of love letters to her.

By 1934 he had decided to marry her and their friendship was much commented on in the foreign press, but Fleet Street was encouraged to ignore the story by the establishment. The British public was kept in the dark about the affair, but it was bound to come out sooner or later. And it did.

King George V died in January 1936 and the Prince of Wales was now Edward VIII.

By the time he had become king, Home Secretary Sir John Simon said Edward was the most widely known and most universally popular personality in the world.

For the future king to want to marry an American was not a good start, and the fact she was shortly to be divorced – for a second time – made it completely unacceptable. This could not be reconciled with his position as head of the Church of England. Furthermore, she was 40, which reduced the likelihood that she would bear children and therefore produce an heir.

Prime Minister Stanley Baldwin spelled this out to Edward in 1936 and gave him an ultimatum – he would have to choose the throne or Wallis Simpson. Edward chose Wallis.

On 10 December 1936, Edward signed the Instrument of Abdication over his wish to marry Mrs Wallis Simpson. Witnessed by all his brothers, it was a simple declaration of his intent to renounce the throne for himself and any of his descendants. He was subsequently created Duke of Windsor.

On the following evening, the former king – now His Royal Highness Prince Edward – broadcast to the nation on the BBC a farewell message written with the help of Winston Churchill.

> You all know the reasons which have impelled me to renounce the Throne. But I want you to understand that in making up my mind I did not forget the country or the Empire which as Prince of Wales, and lately as King, I have for 25 years tried to serve. But you must believe me when I tell you that I have found it impossible to carry the heavy burden of responsibility and to discharge my duties as King as I would wish to do without the help and support of the woman I love.

He then left for France where he married Wallis. They became the Duke and Duchess of Windsor, but to his eternal anger, she was denied the title of Her Royal Highness. Queen Mary was the main mover behind this, backed up by George VI and the Queen Mother. The snub effectively kept the Windsors in exile for the rest of their lives.

The duke and duchess had tea with Adolf Hitler in 1937. 'She would have made a lovely queen,' Hitler said later. With friends like that, who needs enemies? The duke's views on appeasement and the rise of fascism in Germany and Italy led him to be given the role during the Second World War of Governor of the Bahamas, well out of the way of the war effort, amid concerns of German plots to kidnap and use him for propaganda purposes.

The Duke and Duchess of Windsor returned to live in France outside Paris after the war, becoming minor celebrities until his death in 1972. Although he was a royal outcast, his niece Queen Elizabeth II visited him in the final stages of his life and he died of cancer ten days later. He was buried at Frogmore.

GEORGE VI

1895–1952, reigned 1936–1952
Son of George V and Mary of Teck

George VI was the most reluctant of kings. As the second son, he had never expected, nor had he wanted, to take the throne and was furious when his elder brother, Edward, told him he was going to abdicate. 'It isn't possible! It isn't happening!' he shouted when Edward left his brothers on 11 December 1936, and bowed to George on the way out.

When he realised he was going to become king, he told his cousin Lord Louis Mountbatten:

> Dickie, this is absolutely terrible! I never wanted this to happen. I'm quite unprepared for it. David has been trained for this all his life. I've never seen a State paper. I'm only a Naval Officer, it's the only thing I know.

Albert Frederick Arthur George, known in the family as Bertie, was born to George V and Mary during Queen Victoria's reign on 14 December at Sandringham in 1895, on the 34th anniversary of the death of Prince Albert.

He was a shy boy and suffered from a very severe stammer. Naturally left-handed, he was forced to write with his right hand to correct the 'problem'; the stress of this may well have made his stammer, which had begun when he was seven, worse.

He was sent to the Royal Naval College where he came 68th in a class of 68. In 1913 he joined the Navy as a midshipman and in 1916 was a sub-lieutenant on HMS *Collingwood* at the Battle of Jutland. The powers that be looked for safer employment for him and he was appointed to the new Royal Air Force, qualifying as a pilot in 1919. It is sobering to think that 100 years ago, flying in the RAF was adjudged to be safer than sailing on a Royal Navy warship.

In 1920, he was made Duke of York and met Lady Elizabeth Bowes-Lyon who he eventually married in 1923. It was a love match: as Bertie was not heir apparent, there was no great need for an arranged marriage. The marriage was a complete success on all fronts. Elizabeth supported her husband wholeheartedly and the nation took this Scottish commoner (albeit a very posh one) to their hearts.

Lady Elizabeth Bowes-Lyon, daughter of the Earl of Strathmore, was descended from Robert II of Scotland and Owain Glyndwr. One of the Queen Mother's 14th-century ancestors, Sir John Lyon, became Thane of Glamis, and Glamis Castle, the home of Macbeth 300 years before, was the family seat.

She was born and brought up in England and developed into a charming and attractive woman. So worried was she that she would lose all her freedoms if she became the Duchess of York and joined the royal family that Bertie had to propose to her three times before she accepted. At their marriage in 1923, he was 27 and she was 22. They had two children, Elizabeth in 1926, and Margaret in 1930.

⚜ THE KING'S SPEECH

Bertie's stammer rendered public speaking events incredibly stressful. He failed in an attempt to give the closing address at the British Empire Exhibition in 1925. The speech was an ordeal for both the duke and the listeners – his stammering was becoming a major problem. For someone with a stammer, public speaking of any kind, let alone addressing the nation live on radio, is a terrible torture.

But his confidence was slowly beginning to build at this time. He competed at Wimbledon in the 1926 men's doubles tournament, the only member of the royal family ever to do so. His advisor and close friend, naval surgeon Sir Louis Greig, won a place in the tournament and invited the future king to be his doubles partner. It helped to build up an image of a fit and healthy young man but the Wimbledon dream was to end there: they lost in three straight sets.

At about the same time, Bertie's wife, Elizabeth, tracked down an unconventional Australian speech therapist Lionel Logue, who had just set himself up in Harley Street. Bertie and Logue's first meeting was in October 1926.

Logue was seen as something of a quack but his methods, especially those involving breathing and muscle relaxation exercises, certainly seemed to work. All this is memorably and movingly laid out in the 2011 film *The King's Speech*, starring Colin Firth as George VI, Geoffrey Rush as Logue and Helena Bonham Carter as Queen Elizabeth. The film won four Oscars including Best Film and Best Actor (Firth).

George was enjoying the warmth and security of family life, and benefiting from Logue's speech therapy. But all this was shattered by Edward VIII's abdication.

Although his first name was Albert, he took the name of George VI when he became king, not the least as a sign of continuity and stability of the monarchy. The coronation was held on 12 May 1937, the same date as Edward's had been planned, and was broadcast live on radio. It was also an important event in the history of television – it is generally thought that this was the first TV outside broadcast.

The *Daily Mail* said: 'When the King and Queen appeared the picture was so vivid that one felt that this magical television is going to be one of the greatest of all modern inventions.' Well, the *Mail* got that one right.

The return route from Westminster Abbey back to the palace was extended to six miles in length to give as many people as possible the chance to see the new King and Queen. The procession itself was two miles long, and took 40 minutes to pass any one point.

The event was planned as a public spectacle and a celebration of Britain and the Empire and there was a programme of events over three weeks.

The new Queen resented the fact that neither Bertie nor herself had been consulted before the abdication – it fostered a lifelong frostiness towards the Duke and Duchess of Windsor.

George VI's speech to the British Empire on 3 September 1939 at the outbreak of World War Two – portrayed at the climax of *The King's Speech* – was the most important speech of his life. It began:

> In this grave hour, perhaps the most fateful in our history, I send to every household of my peoples, both at home and overseas, this message, spoken with the same depth of feeling for each one of you as if I were able to cross your threshold and speak to you myself.

Logue worked with the King on the text and went to Windsor to hear him deliver it. In a later broadcast, he was impressed to note he made only one mistake: he stumbled over the 'w' in weapons. Afterwards, he asked him why. 'I did it on purpose,' Bertie replied with a grin. 'If I don't make a mistake, people might not know it was me.'

The courage of King George VI and Queen Elizabeth during the Second World War has been well documented. Buckingham Palace was bombed in a daylight raid in 1940 and the King and Queen could have been killed. The Queen characteristically said: 'I'm glad we've been bombed. It makes me feel that I can look the East End in the face.' During the Blitz, the King and Queen visited different parts of London almost daily, inspecting the damage and trying to keep up morale.

When it was suggested that the royal family should leave London and move to a safe place somewhere in the country, the Queen replied defiantly: 'The children won't leave without me; I won't leave without the King; and the King will never leave.'

The King and Winston Churchill had lunch together every Tuesday with no advisers present. In 1944, they both wanted to go along on the D-Day landings but this was vetoed.

When the war ended, on 8 May 1945, Buckingham Palace became the centre of celebrations and the focus for the nation's joy and jubilation; the King and Queen made many appearances on the balcony.

 THE GEORGE CROSS

At the height of the Blitz in September 1940, George VI instituted the George Cross and the George Medal for acts of bravery by civilians. The George Cross takes precedence over all other decorations and medals except for the Victoria Cross. It is the highest gallantry award for civilians. The George Medal is the second level of the decoration and is awarded for 'acts of great bravery'.

In the immediate post-war years, there were many significant developments in all spheres of life. The Labour Government introduced the National Health Service, major industries were nationalised, independence was given to India and the British Empire ceased to exist to be replaced by a Commonwealth of Nations.

In January 1952, George VI saw his daughter Princess Elizabeth and her husband, Philip, off from Heathrow, when they headed out on a tour to East Africa. He returned to Sandringham, and a few days later on 6 February was found dead in his bed. He had been a heavy smoker for many years, ironically encouraged by doctors who thought it would relax his throat and help to cure his stammer. He died of lung cancer aged 57, and is buried at St George's Chapel, Windsor.

ELIZABETH II

Born 1926–, reigned 1952–
Daughter of George VI
and Queen Elizabeth

Princess Elizabeth was in a tree house in a remote part of Kenya when she was told on 6 February 1952, that her father, George VI, had died, and that she would become Queen Elizabeth II. The King had seen Elizabeth and her husband, Philip, off from Heathrow the week before when they flew out on a royal tour to Africa.

She was 25, the same age as Elizabeth I when she ascended the throne, and her reign of 64 years 4 months and 4 days (up to 11 June 2016, her official birthday) is a record. She is the only monarch that the majority of the nation can remember first-hand.

Princess Elizabeth Alexandra Mary was the eldest child of the Duke and Duchess of York. She was born on 21 April 1926, in a private house in Bruton Street, Mayfair, the London home of her mother's parents. She was brought up with her younger sister, Princess Margaret Rose.

There seemed little prospect of her ever acceding to the throne, but Edward's abdication in 1936 changed all that: her father was going to take the throne as George VI, and she became the heir presumptive.

(The heir apparent is an heir whose claim cannot be set aside by the birth of another heir. The heir presumptive is a person whose claim may be set aside by the birth of another heir. In this case, had her parents had a son at some time, he would become the heir.)

When she was six years old, Elizabeth's parents took over Royal Lodge in Windsor Great Park as their own country home. In the grounds of Royal Lodge, Princess Elizabeth had her own small house, Y Bwthyn Bach – it means the Little Cottage – a miniature thatched cottage given to her by the people of Wales in 1932. The cottage had a sitting room, a kitchen with a cooker, and upstairs a bedroom. It was a play den for Elizabeth and Margaret, and their children and their children's children, and later the Queen's great-grandchildren. The house was far more luxurious than most homes at that time.

 FOUR-LEGGED FRIENDS

At the age of seven, a photograph of Elizabeth holding a Pembroke Welsh corgi appeared in the newspapers. The Queen-to-be was to have a lifelong love for the little dogs – a corgi called Susan travelled in the carriage with the newly-weds back to Buckingham Palace after their wedding and then accompanied the royal couple on honeymoon.

The breed was introduced to the royal family by her father King George VI in 1933 when he bought a corgi and named it Dookie (he was, after all, the Duke of York). The animal proved popular with his daughters and was described as 'unquestionably the character of the princesses' delightful canine family' and 'a born sentimentalist'. A second corgi was acquired called Jane who had puppies, two of which, Crackers and Carol, were kept.

For her 18th birthday, Elizabeth was given the corgi called Susan (the one that hitched a ride in the royal wedding carriage) from whom numerous successive dogs were bred. Some corgis were mated with dachshunds (most notably Pipkin, who belonged to Princess Margaret) to create 'dorgis'. At present, the Queen owns two corgis: Willow and Holly and two dorgis: Candy and Vulcan.

Willow and Holly had starring roles, along with the Queen herself and James Bond, as played by Daniel Craig, in the opening sequence of the 2012 London Olympics Opening Ceremony.

The dogs were not universally popular in the royal palaces; members of the household found they could often get in their way, and once, the royal butler Paul Burrell was sent flying by a pack of corgis, much to the enjoyment, it must be said, of most of the royal family. The Princess of Wales called them the 'moving carpet'.

Elizabeth was 13 when the Second World War broke out and lived through the Blitz years at Windsor Castle, although her parents stayed at Buckingham Palace as they had promised. Towards the end of the war, she begged to be allowed to do some sort of national service. She joined the Auxiliary Transport Service and became Second Subaltern Elizabeth Windsor, completing a course in vehicle maintenance.

Much to her father's disapproval, Elizabeth fell for the first boy she properly met – she was only 13 when she met her third cousin, Philip of Greece, who was 18, the grandson of King George of the Hellenes. She had eyes for nobody else. King George VI had nothing against the good-looking naval officer but like all fathers, he wanted to make sure that the couple were serious about the future.

The King eventually gave in but insisted that Elizabeth was over 21 before becoming betrothed and a few weeks after her birthday, the couple were engaged.

Elizabeth was already preparing for queenship. In a remarkably mature radio broadcast in 1947 on her 21st birthday, she said: 'I declare before you all, that my whole life, whether it be long or short, shall be devoted to your service and the service of our great imperial family to which we all belong.'

Well, that was, incredibly, almost 70 years ago, and she has been as good as her word.

The wedding took place in front of 2,000 guests at Westminster Abbey on 20 November 1947, and the radio broadcast attracted more than 200 million listeners around the world. Elizabeth's dress was partly made of material bought with clothing coupons.

The couple lived for a while in Malta where Philip was serving with the Navy. As George VI's illness worsened, Elizabeth and Philip were drawn into more and more royal duties. In the last years of George's reign, they performed an increasing number of public duties (at home and abroad) and toured Canada, Australia and New Zealand.

Queen Elizabeth and Philip's first child, Prince Charles, was born in 1948 – so the matter of the succession was assured. There was an heir apparent in the first year of marriage.

PRINCE PHILIP

Philip was brought up by his British relatives on his mother's side, the Mountbattens. In 1939, he started studying at Dartmouth and served with distinction in the Royal Navy in the war. He took British nationality after the war as Lieutenant Philip Mountbatten and was created Duke of Edinburgh on his wedding day. He took the title of Prince Philip at the suggestion of Prime Minister Harold Macmillan in 1957.

 ## THE CORONATION

It was Elizabeth herself, against the advice of her counsellors, including the prime minister Sir Winston Churchill, who pressed for the coronation in Westminster Abbey, on 2 June 1953, to be televised.

She was young and clearly saw that television was the medium of the future. She wanted to be as close as she could to her subjects. In the early 1950s, television was a novelty and few people had TV sets. But in what was a great boost for television manufacturers and also the BBC, thousands of people clamoured to buy a black-and-white set to watch the event on a tiny screen.

She was the 39th sovereign to be crowned in Westminster Abbey, where the ceremony was watched by 8,000 guests. Millions more around the world watched as the BBC set up their biggest-ever outside broadcast to provide live coverage of the event on radio and television. An estimated 20 million people in Britain watched the ceremony on TV. Street parties were held throughout the UK as people crowded round to watch the ceremony.

An estimated 3 million people lined the streets of London to catch a glimpse of the new monarch as she made her way from Buckingham Palace to Westminster Abbey and back in the Gold State Coach.

On her way to the Abbey, the Queen wore the George IV State Diadem, which was made for George IV's coronation in 1820. The diadem features 1,333 diamonds and 169 pearls, all of which were originally hired for the early coronations. It has taken on a historic symbolism and has become an iconic royal image – the Queen wears the diadem on all coins and all stamps produced during her reign.

The Queen's dress, designed by Norman Hartnell, was made of white satin embroidered at her suggestion with the emblems of the UK – rose, thistle, leek and shamrock – and also the Commonwealth. Its exquisite embroidery in gold and silver and pastel-coloured silks was encrusted with seed pearls and crystals to create a lattice-work effect.

Elizabeth sat in King Edward's Chair, made in 1300 for Edward I and used at every coronation since. She was crowned with St Edward's Crown, made of solid gold and weighing 2.23 kg (4 lb 12 oz – equivalent to almost two and a quarter bags of sugar). The Queen was said to have worn the crown round Buckingham Palace to get used to it, even feeding the corgis wearing it.

The crown in its current form was made in 1661 and first used by Charles II, having been refurbished from an older crown. There is speculation that the lower part might be from Edward the Confessor's crown dating from 1042.

ON TOP OF THE WORLD

On 29 May 1953, two climbers from the British Mount Everest Expedition, New Zealander Edmund Hillary and Nepalese Sherpa Tensing Norgay became the first people to climb Everest. They reached the summit after a gruelling climb up the north face. It was the ninth international attempt to climb the 29,028 feet mountain.

The Times newspaper had sponsored the expedition led by Col John Hunt and their correspondent on the spot, James Morris, had to make sure that his paper broke the story. He heard the news at base camp the next day and then made a swift and hazardous descent down the mountain with the news.

He sent a coded message by runner to Namche Bazaar 20 miles away, where a wireless transmitter was used to forward it as a telegram to the British Embassy in Kathmandu.

The conquest of Everest was probably the last major news story to be delivered to the world by runner. Morris's encoded message to his paper read: 'Snow Conditions Bad. Stop. Advance Base Abandoned Yesterday. Stop. Awaiting Improvement. All Well.'

Snow Conditions Bad was the agreed code to signify that the summit had been reached. *Advance Base Abandoned* referred to Hillary and *Awaiting Improvement* referred to Sherpa Tenzing. This was received and understood in London in time for the news to be released, by happy coincidence, on the morning of the coronation on 2 June.

DID YOU KNOW?

Coronation chicken was invented for the foreign guests to be entertained at the coronation. The food was prepared in advance, and cookery writer Constance Spry proposed a recipe of cold chicken in a creamy curry sauce. Spry's recipe won the approval of the Minister of Works and has since been known as coronation chicken.

 PRINCESS MARGARET

Princess Margaret (1930–2002) was Queen Elizabeth's younger sister and second in line to the throne.

She first met Group Captain Peter Townsend when he chaperoned the two princesses on a visit of South Africa in 1947. He was 16 years older than Margaret and had two children but Margaret fell in love with him. He was an equerry to George VI and on the King's death, became Comptroller of the Queen Mother's household.

Townsend was divorced in 1952 and Margaret declared her wish to marry, but it was opposed by her mother, Queen Elizabeth, the Queen Mother, the church, the Cabinet and the prime minister, Winston Churchill, on the grounds that he was a divorcee.

Under the Royal Marriages Act of 1772, the princess needed the Queen's permission to marry before the age of 25. After that, she also needed Parliament's approval.

The episode rumbled on for some time until Margaret said in October 1955 that she had decided not to marry Group Capt Townsend. She issued a statement:

I would like it to be known that I have decided not to marry Group Captain Peter Townsend. I have been aware that, subject to my renouncing my rights of succession, it might have been possible for me to contract a civil marriage.

But mindful of the Church's teaching that Christian marriage is indissoluble and conscious of my duty to the Commonwealth, I have resolved to put these considerations before any others.

The statement was deemed so important at the time that the BBC interrupted its normal programmes to broadcast the news.

In 1960, she married Antony Armstrong-Jones, a society photographer, and the couple were created the Earl and Countess of Snowdon. They had two children, David and Sarah.

 AND ANOTHER THING...

Later in the decade, in 1969, in front of 4,000 guests inside the walls of Caernarfon Castle, the Investiture of Prince Charles as Prince of Wales took place, when he was aged 20 and at a time of growing Welsh nationalism. The ceremony at the castle, where the first investiture had been held in 1300, went off without incident. It was a global televisual event with a worldwide audience of 500 million.

Charles had studied some Welsh and Welsh history during a term at the University College of Wales, Aberystwyth, earlier that year and made speeches in both English and Welsh.

YOUR MAJESTY? HER MAJESTY

The relationship between the Queen and the Queen Mother was a close one. They regularly talked on the telephone in the morning, often discussing the day's racing ahead. The highlight of the day for one Palace telephone operator was when she connected the Queen and the Queen Mother with the words: 'Your Majesty? Her Majesty, Your Majesty.'

THE SILVER JUBILEE, 1977

The Queen's Silver Jubilee in 1977 was marked with celebrations throughout the country and the Commonwealth.

During the summer, the Queen undertook a large-scale tour. No other sovereign could have visited so much of Britain in a three-month period. The tours covered 36 counties – Glasgow saw the biggest crowds the city had ever seen, and on one day in Lancashire, it was estimated that more than a million people turned out to see her.

Overseas visits were made to Western Samoa, Australia, New Zealand, Tonga, Tasmania, Papua New Guinea, Canada and the West Indies. The Queen and the Duke of Edinburgh must have uttered a huge sigh of relief when it was over – it was estimated that they travelled 56,000 miles in the year.

On 7 June, vast crowds saw the Queen process to St Paul's Cathedral in the Gold State Coach, which had last been used at her coronation. Afterwards at a lunch at the Guildhall, the Queen made a speech:

My Lord Mayor, when I was twenty-one I pledged my life to the service of our people and I asked for God's help to make good that vow. Although that vow was made in my salad days, when I was green in judgment, I do not regret nor retract one word of it.

An estimated 500 million people watched on television as the procession returned down The Mall.

 LORD MOUNTBATTEN

Lord Louis Mountbatten, the Queen's cousin, was murdered by the IRA in August 1979 while holidaying in Mullaghmore, County Sligo. His grandson Nicholas, aged 14, was also killed, along with a local boy who worked on the boats when the terrorists detonated a bomb and blew up the family fishing boat.

The Queen was close to Mountbatten and had started married life in 1947 staying at his home in Malta. In 2012, she visited Belfast and shook hands with the alleged former Provisional IRA Commander Martin McGuinness in what was a massive step of reconciliation. It was certainly one of the most significant moments of her long reign.

🌸 THE 1980S: FAIRY-TALE WEDDINGS AND CONFLICT IN THE FALKLANDS

The 1980s started well for the Queen and the royal family. The friendship between Prince Charles and Lady Diana Spencer blossomed in 1980 and Charles proposed to her in the nursery at Windsor Castle in February 1981. She was 20 and he was 32.

Lady Diana Spencer had been born at Park House next to the Queen's Sandringham estate, and was the youngest daughter of Viscount Althorp and his wife, Frances. She was the first British citizen to marry an heir to the British throne in 300 years.

The royal wedding on 29 July 1981, at St Paul's Cathedral was one of those memorable broadcasting events, described as the 'fairy tale wedding' and the 'wedding of the century' and was watched by 750 million people worldwide, a television record. There were 3,500 guests in the cathedral. Two million people lined the route of the procession from Clarence House.

Diana's wedding dress was made of ivory silk taffeta, decorated with lace, hand embroidery, sequins and 10,000 pearls. It was designed by Elizabeth and David Emanuel and had a 25-foot train of ivory taffeta and antique lace.

A national holiday was declared – it was a zenith in the life of the royal family.

The princess gave birth to Prince William at St Mary's Hospital, London, on 21 June 1982 – the matter of the succession had been quickly settled. He was the first heir to the throne born in a hospital. He was christened William Arthur Philip Louis Windsor and there was some controversy in the media at the time when she decided to take him on her first major overseas visit to Australia and New Zealand soon after.

The Prince and Princess of Wales's second son, Henry Charles Albert David, was born on September 15, 1984. His official title is Prince Henry of Wales: the birth announcement said, 'Prince

Henry... to be known as Harry.' He is universally known as Prince Harry. At the time of his birth he was third in line of succession but is now fifth behind Prince George and Princess Charlotte.

In 1982, the UK went to war with Argentina over the Falkland Islands. The Queen and Prince Philip had a very personal interest in the war – Prince Andrew, their second son, was a helicopter pilot in the conflict.

Argentina had invaded the Falkland Islands in April of 1982 claiming they belonged to them. Prime Minister Margaret Thatcher ordered a task force of 100 ships and 27,000 personnel to be sent to the South Atlantic to take the back the islands. The conflict was short-lived and ended when Port Stanley was taken back in June.

By all accounts, Prince Andrew had more than one close shave, especially when his Sea King helicopter was used as a decoy to attract Argentinian Exocet missiles away from Royal Navy ships.

Prince Andrew married Sarah Ferguson at Westminster Abbey in July 1986 in another massively popular royal wedding. An estimated 500 million people watched worldwide on television, and a crowd of 100,000 gathered outside Buckingham Palace to greet the newly-wed couple.

⚜ AN *ANNUS HORRIBILIS* IN A DIFFICULT DECADE

If the 1970s and 1980s were generally happy times for the Royal Family the 1990s were the opposite, and the year 1992 was singled out as the stand-out worst year of Queen Elizabeth II's reign.

The Queen called 1992 her *annus horribilis*. Events in the year included the break-up of the marriage of Prince Andrew and the Duchess of York; one month later, Princess Anne divorced her husband, Capt Mark Phillips; a biography revealed the rifts in the marriage of Prince Charles and the Princess of Wales; the affair between Prince Charles and Camilla Parker Bowles was revealed; and on 20 November, Windsor Castle, the largest inhabited castle in the world, was seriously damaged by a fierce fire.

The fire started in the Queen's private chapel in the northeast wing when a curtain pressed against a spotlight burst into flames, causing a massive blaze. Damage ran into millions of pounds: nine rooms were completely gutted and another 100 were damaged in the fire.

The Queen and the Duke of York, who was in the Castle at the time, helped to rescue priceless works of art from the royal collection. It took 250 firefighters 12 hours to put out the blaze. St George's Hall was badly damaged, and Brunswick Tower was completely destroyed.

The castle is owned by the British Government, not the royal family, and the issue of who was to pay for the repairs became a matter for public and political debate. The restoration cost £40 million and was completed after five years in November 1997. The Queen contributed £2 million to the restoration and agreed to start paying income tax from 1993 onwards. (In 2015, the Queen and the royal family received £35.7 million from the Sovereign Grant. Sir Alan Reid, Keeper of the Privy Purse, said the royal family continued to give excellent value for money – the grant works out at 56p per head of the population per year.)

The Queen made a famous speech at the Lord Mayor's dinner at the Mansion House towards the end of that year:

> 1992 is not a year on which I shall look back with undiluted pleasure. In the words of one of my more sympathetic correspondents, it has turned out to be an *annus horribilis*.

I suspect that I am not alone in thinking it so. Indeed, I suspect that there are very few people or institutions unaffected by these last months of worldwide turmoil and uncertainty.

This generosity and whole-hearted kindness of the Corporation of the City to Prince Philip and me would be welcome at any time, but at this particular moment, in the aftermath of Friday's tragic fire at Windsor, it is especially so.

(Sir Edward Ford, the Queen's assistant private secretary, was later revealed to be the 'sympathetic correspondent'.)

But she had not lost her sense of humour. She said:

It is possible to have too much of a good thing. A well-meaning Bishop was obviously doing his best when he told Queen Victoria: 'Ma'am, we cannot pray too often, nor too fervently, for the Royal Family.' The Queen's reply was: 'Too fervently, no; too often, yes.' I, like Queen Victoria, have always been a believer in that old maxim, 'Moderation in all things'.

Charles and Diana's marriage fell apart in the early 1990s. The Prince of Wales had resumed his affair with Camilla Parker Bowles and later Diana began a relationship with Major James Hewitt.

In December 1992, Prime Minister John Major announced in the Commons the couple's 'amicable separation'.

Prince Charles confirmed his affair with Camilla Parker Bowles in a TV interview with Jonathan Dimbleby in June 1994. The following year, in November, the Princess of Wales was the subject of an interview on the BBC with Martin Bashir. Referring to her husband's affair with Camilla Parker Bowles, she famously said: 'Well, there were three of us in this marriage, so it was a bit crowded.'

In December 1995, it was announced that the Queen had sent letters to the Prince and Princess of Wales advising them to divorce. The divorce was finalised in August 1996 – Diana reportedly received a lump sum of £15 million and an allowance of £400,000 a year.

In a tragic turn of events that shocked the world, Diana was killed in a car crash in Paris on 31 August 1997, in which her companion, Dodi Fayed, and the driver were also killed.

The news was not released officially until 4.40 am and an incredulous nation awoke on the Sunday morning to learn the sensational news. The sudden violent death of such a popular and young royal princess set off an extraordinary explosion of public emotion.

People left flowers, candles, cards and messages by their thousands in front of the gates at Kensington Palace, spreading out as far as Kensington High Street. Tens of thousands of people visited the pop-up shrine.

The royal family were at Balmoral at the time, and stayed there. This, along with the fact that it took a few days for the flag to be lowered to half-mast at Buckingham Palace, was seen as unfeeling and damaged the reputation of the royal family for a time.

Diana's funeral took place a week later on 6 September. The funeral procession left Kensington Palace with Princes William, aged 15, and Harry, aged 12, walking behind the coffin along with Prince Charles, the Duke of Edinburgh and Diana's brother, Charles Spencer, 9th Earl Spencer.

The princess was buried privately the same day. A set of rosary beads was placed in her hands, a gift she had received from Mother Teresa who had died in the same week as Diana. Diana's grave is on a small island in the middle of the ornamental lake at the family seat, Althorp.

In 1999, *Time* magazine named Diana one of the 100 Most Important People of the 20th Century.

Prince Charles married Camilla Parker Bowles in a civil ceremony at Windsor Guildhall on 9 April 2005. HRH the Duchess of Cornwall will be known as the Princess Consort when Charles takes the throne.

⚜ THE GOLDEN JUBILEE, 2002

The Queen's Golden Jubilee year in 2002 started on a sad note for her – her sister and her mother both died in quick succession. Princess Margaret, Countess of Snowdon, once vivacious and glamorous, died of a stroke in hospital on 9 February 2002, aged 71.

A month and a half later, on 30 March, Queen Elizabeth, the Queen Mother, died in her sleep at her home, the Royal Lodge in Windsor Great Park, the Queen at her bedside. She was 101 years old and at the time of her death, was the longest living member of Britain's royal family. The coffin was taken to Westminster Hall so the public could pay their respects. Princess Margaret's ashes were interred with the Queen Mother's coffin in the George VI Chapel at Windsor.

Later in 2002, in June, the Queen could start to celebrate her Golden Jubilee, 50 years on the throne. The last monarch to celebrate a Golden Jubilee before her was Queen Victoria.

The Queen and the Duke of Edinburgh undertook another massive tour and were on the road for most of May, June and July. They visited 70 cities and towns in the UK in 50 counties. The Queen and the duke circumnavigated the globe during the year, starting with visits to Jamaica, New Zealand and Australia. The 2002 tour was the sixth time that the Queen travelled around the world on a single tour.

One million people gathered in The Mall to watch the Jubilee festivities on 3 and 4 June. People around Britain held street parties, garden parties and other events to celebrate the Golden Jubilee.

In a replica of events at Victoria's Golden Jubilee in 1887, a chain of beacons and bonfires was lit across the UK from Land's End to John O'Groats and from Great Yarmouth to Holyhead, and in the Arctic Circle and Antarctica as well as throughout the Commonwealth, as a climax to the day's festivities. The Queen lit the National Beacon in The Mall. The beacons formed a chain across the UK.

 GOLDEN MOMENTS: HIGHLIGHTS FROM THE GOLDEN JUBILEE CELEBRATIONS

One of the highlights of the four-day celebrations was a remarkable equestrian spectacular at Windsor Castle, aptly titled 'All the Queen's Horses', featuring 1,000 horses and 2,000 people in an event that stretched over three days.

The finale of the show was a recreation of the 1953 coronation procession, which featured the Gold Stage Coach pulled by eight Windsor grey horses.

Horses are the Queen's great love and passion, and she always attends the Derby and Royal Ascot and still rides out at the age of 90.

The Queen was the first member of the royal family to be awarded a gold disc from the recording industry: 100,000 copies of the CD of *The Party at the Palace* were sold in the first week of its release. The pop concert itself was one of the most watched in history, attracting around 200 million viewers all over the world. There was another Queen at the palace that night: the rock group Queen, whose lead guitarist Brian May famously played 'God Save the Queen' from the roof of the palace to start the concert off.

Twenty-seven aircraft flew over Buckingham Palace for the finale of the Jubilee weekend celebrations. The flypast ended with Concorde and the Red Arrows trailing red, white and blue.

⚜ THE DIAMOND JUBILEE, 2012

In 2012, the Queen celebrated her Diamond Jubilee – and the world celebrated with her.

The Thames Diamond Jubilee Pageant revived a tradition that dated back more than 400 years. Around 1,000 boats from across the UK, the Commonwealth and around the world sailed down the Thames. The Royal Barge, decorated in red and gold and which carried the Queen and the Duke of Edinburgh, led the flotilla.

A network of 2,012 beacons was lit by communities and individuals throughout the United Kingdom, as well as the Channel Islands, the Isle of Man and the Commonwealth. As in 2002, the Queen lit the National Beacon. In July, the Queen opened the Commonwealth Games in Manchester. Members of the royal family visited every realm, as well as other Commonwealth countries and crown dependencies.

A rock concert was held outside Buckingham Palace on 4 June 4, 2012, with a stellar cast including Cliff Richard, Paul McCartney, Elton John, Shirley Bassey, Kylie Minogue, Stevie Wonder and Tom Jones. The group Madness played 'Our House' from the roof of the palace, changing the words of one line, in deference to the Queen, to: 'Our house... in the middle of one's street.'

The Queen and the Duke of Edinburgh celebrated their blue sapphire 65th wedding anniversary on 19 November 2012. It is almost certain that she did not send herself a congratulatory message but she should have done. It is the longest lasting royal marriage and is a record that may well stand forever.

⚜ AN IMPRESSIVE TRACK RECORD

It is said that the Queen is the most famous woman in the world. There are not many people after all whose portrait is featured on 28 billion coins, which was the number in circulation in the UK in 2014. And also 3,421 billion bank notes (value £67 billion).

On 9 September 2015, Queen Elizabeth became the longest reigning monarch surpassing Victoria's reign of 63 years and seven months. She retains her sense of humour. Somebody in the street said that she looked like the Queen. 'That's reassuring,' she replied.

The Queen meets her prime minister once a week at Buckingham Palace. Over the years, she has had dealings with 13 prime ministers, starting with Winston Churchill through to Theresa May. She seems to have had particularly good relationships with two Labour leaders, Harold Wilson and James Callaghan. No written record of the meetings is ever taken; government papers are delivered to her in the famous Red Boxes, which she assiduously studies every day.

DID YOU KNOW?

The Queen celebrates two birthdays each year – her real birthday on 21 April, and her official birthday on a Saturday early in June.

She usually spends her real birthday privately, but is joined by other members of the royal family for Trooping the Colour (also known as the Queen's Birthday Parade) for her official birthday.

⚜ A DAY TO REMEMBER

The weekend of 11 June 2016 marked the Queen's official 90th birthday. On Friday 10 June, there was a National Service of Thanksgiving at St Paul's Cathedral. That date was Prince Philip's 95th birthday, and the event, celebrating her birthday and not his, seemed to be a metaphor for the way her husband has supported the Queen in an understated way throughout their 68 years of marriage.

Fifty-three members of the extended Royal Family attended the service in a massive show of support for the Queen. There were so many, in fact, that some of them travelled from Buckingham Palace and back in minibuses, rather than the traditional limousines.

The Queen's Birthday Honours were announced on this day and Tim Peake, the astronaut, was still on the International Space Station when he was awarded a CMG – Companion of the Most Distinguished Order of St Michael and St George. This honour is awarded solely for achievement outside the UK; in this instance, 'for extraordinary service beyond our planet'.

Large crowds turned out for Trooping the Colour, the Queen's official Birthday Parade, on the Saturday, and flocked down the Mall after the procession. The newspapers were united in saying that the Duke and Duchess of Cambridge's 13-month-old daughter Princess Charlotte stole the show making her debut on the balcony and waving to the flypast of 29 aircraft.

On the Sunday, around 10,000 people sat down to a picnic lunch on the Mall – The Patrons' Lunch – to which all of the 612 charities that are connected to the Queen were invited.

The weather was inclement but that did not seem to dampen the traditional British and royal spirits: *Long to rain over us, God Save the Queen.*

⚜ THE QUEEN IN NUMBERS

3,500,000 letters and emails answered during her reign. (Not clear how many people were involved in the counting, or the writing.)

540,000 couples congratulated on Diamond Wedding anniversaries

400,000 honours conferred at more than 600 investitures

175,000 telegrams sent to people celebrating their 100th birthdays

50,000 people hosted at receptions, banquets, lunches, dinners and garden parties at Buckingham Palace in an average year

3,500 Acts of Parliament to which she has given royal assent

600 charities and organisations of which she is patron

306 engagements in the UK in 2015

250 official visits made overseas

117 countries visited during her reign

53 countries in the Commonwealth

37 Royal Variety Performances she has been forced to endure

16 visits to Australia

⚜ THE QUEEN AND PRINCE PHILIP'S CHILDREN

1. Prince Charles Philip Arthur George, Prince of Wales, *1st in line*
Born 14 November 1948, at Buckingham Palace
Married Lady Diana Spencer, born 1 July 1961; died 31 August
    1997, in Paris
Divorced 28 August 1996

**Issue 1: Prince William Arthur Philip Louis, Duke of Cambridge,
    *2nd in line***
Born 21 June 1982, at St Mary's Hospital, Paddington
Married Catherine Middleton, born 9 January 1982
Styled Prince William of Wales

William and Kate's issue:
1. Prince George of Cambridge, *3rd in line*
Born 22 July 2013, at St Mary's Hospital, Paddington

2. Princess Charlotte of Cambridge, *4th in line*
Born 2 May 2015, at St Mary's Hospital, Paddington

**Issue 2: Prince Henry Charles Albert David (Prince Harry),
    *5th in line***
Born 15 September 1984, at St Mary's Hospital, Paddington
Styled Prince Henry of Wales

**2. Princess Anne Elizabeth Alice Louise, the Princess Royal,
    *12th in line***
Born 15 August 1950, at Clarence House
Married Captain Mark Phillips, born 22 September 1948
Divorced 1992
Married Commander Timothy Laurence, born 1 March 1955

Issue 1: Peter Phillips, born 15 November 1977, *13th in line*
Married Autumn Kelly, born 3 May 1978

Peter and Autumn's issue:
1. Savannah, born 29 December 2010, *14th in line*

2. Isla, born 29 March 2012, *15th in line*

Issue 2: Zara Phillips, born 15 May 1981 *16th in line*
Married Mike Tindall, born 18 October 1978

Zara and Mike's issue:
1. Mia Tindall, born 17 January 2014, *17th in line*

3. Prince Andrew Albert Christian Edward, Duke of York,
   6th in line
Born 16 February 1960, at Buckingham Palace
Married Sarah Ferguson, born 15 October 1959
Divorced on 30 May 1996

Issue 1: Princess Beatrice Elizabeth Mary, born 8 August 1988,
   7th in line

Issue 2: Princess Eugenie Victoria Helena, born 23 March 1990,
   8th in line

4. Prince Edward Antony Richard Louis, Earl of Wessex,
   9th in line
Born 10 March 1964, at Buckingham Palace
Married Sophie Rhys-Jones, born 20 January 1965

Issue 1: Lady Louise Windsor, born 8 November 2003,
  11th in line

Issue 2: James, Viscount Severn, born 17 December 2007, *10th in line*

⚜ THE ORDER OF SUCCESSION

The Act of Settlement 1701 laid down that only Protestant heirs of Princess Sophia of Hanover, granddaughter of James I, could succeed to the British throne. Under common law, the crown was passed on by male primogeniture. The crown passed from the monarch to the eldest son. If the monarch did not have a son, the crown passed to the eldest daughter. If the monarch had a number of sons, they all took precedence over any daughters, irrespective of age. And the sons' children took precedence too.

This all changed in 2015 with the Succession to the Crown Act. Absolute primogeniture was introduced and persons born after 28 October 2011 are henceforth ranked retrospectively in age order, regardless of sex.

In 2013, Prince William and Catherine, the Duke and Duchess of Cambridge, had a baby, George, who is now 3rd in line of succession. In 2015, they had a second child, Charlotte, who became 4th in line of succession by right and cannot be pushed down the order at a later date were her parents to have another son (or sons).

In the order of succession at the start of 2013, Prince Harry was 3rd in line but he has been pushed down to 5th by Prince William's children. In the latest list, Prince Andrew is 6th and his daughters, Beatrice and Eugene are 7th and 8th respectively. Prince Edward, the Queen's youngest son, is 9th in line and his children, James and Louise, 10th and 11th. Lord Severn takes precedence over his elder sister, Louise, because he is male.

Princess Anne is preceded in the list by her younger brothers, Andrew and Edward (and their children), because they are male.

Princess Anne's son, Peter Phillips, is 13th in line, and Savannah and Isla, his young daughters, are 14th and 15th. Princess Anne's daughter, Zara, comes 16th and Mia Grace, Zara's daughter with former England rugby union star Mike Tindall, is 17th.

The 2015 Act removed the disqualification of those who marry Roman Catholics.

A genealogist prepares a list of the royal succession every ten years. The last list was prepared in 2011. There were 5,753 names on the list then – the British throne is not going to disappear for lack of qualified candidates for the job.

The last person on the list – 5,753rd in line – is Karin Vogel, a therapist from Rostock, Germany. She will not be lying in bed at night wondering if she will ever get the call. On the law of averages, the first three on the list, Charles, William and George should see the next 75 years out.

The course of history could have been different if the eldest daughter had succeeded to the throne at the beginning of the 20th century. Queen Victoria's eldest child was Victoria, who went on to marry Frederick III, Emperor of Germany and King of Prussia. Their eldest son became Kaiser Wilhelm II. Had the young Victoria succeeded her mother, it is possible that Kaiser Wilhelm, the German Emperor generally blamed for starting the First World War, could have acceded to the British throne.

AFTERWORD

Just in case you need any help remembering the monarchs covered in this book, this long-standing classic rhyming mnemonic will secure in your memory the Kings and Queens of England from William the Conqueror in 1066. (For the Saxon and Danish kings, I'm afraid you'll need to work out your own poem!)

Willie, Willie, Harry, Steve,
Harry, Dick, John, Harry Three;
One, Two, Three Neds, Richard Two,
Harry Four, Five, Six... then who?
Edward Four, Five, Dick the Bad,
Harrys twain and Ned Six the Lad,
Mary, Bessie, James the Vain,
Charlie, Charlie, James again.
William and Mary, Anna Gloria,
Four Georges, William and Victoria,
Edward Seven next, and then
George the Fifth in 1910.
Ned the Eighth soon abdicated,
Then George the Sixth was coronated;
After which Elizabeth,
And that's all, folks, until her death.

ACKNOWLEDGMENTS

My main thanks are due to the historians, most of them anonymous here, who have gone before me. I have sat on their shoulders and would not have been able to do this book without them.

Phil Lloyd displayed a deep knowledge on some periods and was very supportive throughout. Glyn and Sue Evans were also very knowledgeable and helpful.

I must also acknowledge the help I have received from the people at Summersdale Publishers. Telephone conversations with my editor, Abbie Headon, were something I looked forward to and she made many good points to improve the text. Later, Emma Grundy Haigh was helpful, before Chris Turton took over the task of producing the book. Thanks to them. All mistakes are mine alone.

The family deserves credit for putting up with me writing another book. My wife, Bethan, has taken the meaning of long-suffering to a new level.

SELECT BIBLIOGRAPHY

This book will possibly have triggered further interest in the history of England and the Royal Family. Thousands of books have been written on the subject.

A good reference book on the monarchy is *Britain's Royal Families: the Complete Genealogy* by Alison Weir, which includes a good section on the kings and queens of Scotland. It also includes a lengthy select bibliography. Anything by Alison Weir is worth reading.

The Mammoth Book of British Kings and Queens, by Mike Ashley, is what it says on the cover – a massive and detailed reference book that is especially good on the Welsh and Scottish kingdoms.

The Lives of the Kings and Queens of England, edited by Antonia Fraser, is a well-illustrated, long-standing, accessible work of reference.

A number of excellent biographies have been written on Elizabeth II: by Ben Pimlott, Robert Lacey, Andrew Marr and Robert Hardman, among others.

I also enjoyed the superior popular general histories of England, by Robert Lacey, *Great Tales from English History*, and Simon Jenkins, *A Short History of England*.

The English and their History, by Robert Tombs is a massive and scholarly 1,000-page tome (a large heavy book) that manages to be definitive and beautifully written at the same time.

FOR THE LOVE OF
SHAKESPEARE

A COMPANION

BETH MILLER

FOR THE LOVE OF SHAKESPEARE

Beth Miller

ISBN: 978-1-84953-925-8

Hardback

£9.99

There's never been a better time to take a fresh look at William Shakespeare's eternal works. A treasure trove of wit, imagination and emotion, his plays and poems continue to surprise, inspire, console and delight us. Whether you're a lifelong lover of the Bard or a curious newcomer to his world, this companion will lift the curtain on the unforgettable characters and stories of Britain's greatest dramatist.

'*Well informed, wide-ranging, undogmatic and reader-friendly, this agreeably written book offers a highly accessible and enticing guide to Shakespeare's life, his writings, and his impact, which will give pleasure to those who already enjoy the plays and poems and may well help others to see what they are missing.*'

Sir Stanley Wells

FOR THE LOVE OF
RADIO 4

AN UNOFFICIAL
COMPANION

CAROLINE HODGSON

FOR THE LOVE OF RADIO 4

Caroline Hodgson

ISBN: 978-1-84953-642-4

Hardback

£9.99

From *Farming Today* at sunrise to the gentle strains of 'Sailing By' and the Shipping Forecast long after midnight, Radio 4 provides the soundtrack to life for millions of Britons. In *For the Love of Radio 4*, Caroline Hodgson celebrates all that's best about the nation's favourite spoken-word station, taking us on a tour through its history, its key personalities and programmes, and countless memorable moments from the archives.

'I found the book to be full of fascinating detail. It is clearly a labour of love, perfectly designed for Radio 4 lovers.'

Simon Brett

'If you love Radio 4 it's impossible to turn it off. If you read this book it's impossible to put down.'

Charles Collingwood

A CELEBRATION OF THE
WORLD'S FINEST MUSIC

FOR THE LOVE OF
CLASSICAL
MUSIC

A COMPANION

CAROLINE HIGH

FOR THE LOVE OF CLASSICAL MUSIC

Caroline High

ISBN: 978-1-84953-732-2

Hardback

£9.99

From Bach to Beethoven, Vivaldi to Vaughan Williams, the world
of classical music has something to enchant every listener. Whether
you're an armchair connoisseur, a regular concert-goer or an
ardent musician, *For the Love of Classical Music* will take you
on a tour encompassing landmark pieces and performances, key
artists and composers, and surprising facts about the world's most
beautiful music.

FOR THE LOVE OF
THE
ARCHERS

AN UNOFFICIAL
COMPANION

BETH MILLER

FOR THE LOVE OF THE ARCHERS

Beth Miller

ISBN: 978-1-84953-773-5

Hardback

£9.99

It's been over 60 years since the familiar dum-di-dum-di-dum-di-dum of 'Barwick Green' first brought The Archers to our airwaves, and in that time millions of listeners have followed the everyday lives of country folk in Ambridge. This new companion, which brings together facts and trivia about characters, controversies and country customs in one handy volume, will delight avid addicts and keen newbies alike.

If you're interested in finding out more about our
books, find us on Facebook at **Summersdale Publishers**
and follow us on Twitter at **@Summersdale**.

www.summersdale.com